Fly Fishing Montana

A No Nonsense Guide to Top Waters

Brian & Jenny Grossenbacher

Brian Grossenbacher at the Boulder River on a summer day.
Photo by Jenny Grossenbacher.

NO NONSENSE
Tucson, Arizona

**Fly Fishing
Montana**

A No Nonsense Guide to Top Waters
ISBN-10 1-892469-14-6
ISBN-13 978-1-892469-14-4
ISBN-13 978-1-61881-117-2 (ebook)

© 2007 Brian & Jenny Grossenbacher

Published by:
No Nonsense Fly Fishing Guidebooks
P.O. Box 91858
Tucson, AZ 85752-1858
(520) 547-2462
www.nononsenseguides.com

2 3 4 5 6   15 14 13 12

Printed in USA

Editor: Howard Fisher
Maps, Illustrations, Design & Production:
Pete Chadwell, Dynamic Arts
Front Cover: Photo by Brian Grossenbacher
Back Cover: Photo by Brian Grossenbacher

The No Nonsense Creed

The best way to go fly fishing is to find out a little something about a water, then just go there. Experimentation, trial-and-error, wrong turns, surprises, self-reliance, and new discoveries, even in familiar waters, are what make the memories. The next best way is to learn enough from a local to save you from going too far wrong. You still find the water on your own, and it still feels as if you were the first to do so.

This is the idea for our unique No Nonsense fly fishing series. Our books reveal little hush-hush information, yet they give all you need to find what will become your own secret places.

Painstakingly pared down, our writing is elegantly simple. Each title offers a local fly fishing expert's candid tour of his or her favorite fly fishing waters. Nothing is oversold or out of proportion. Everything is authentic, especially the discoveries and experiences you get after using our books. In his outstanding book Jerusalem Creek, Ted Leeson echoes our idea: "Discovering a new trout stream is a wonderful thing, and even if its whereabouts are common knowledge, to come upon the place yourself for the first time is nonetheless true discovery."

Where No Nonsense Guides Come From

No Nonsense guidebooks give you a quick, clear understanding of the essential information needed to fly fish a region's most outstanding waters. The authors are highly experienced and qualified local fly fishers. Maps are tidy versions of the author's sketches. These guides are produced by the fly fishers, their friends, and spouses of fly fishers, at No Nonsense Fly Fishing Guidebooks.

All who produce No Nonsense guides believe in providing top quality products at a reasonable price. We also believe all information should be verified. We never hesitate to go out, fly rod in hand, to verify the facts and figures that appear in the pages of these guides. The staff is committed to this research.

It's hard work, but we're glad to do it for you.

Jenny Grossenbacher with a healthy brown on DePuy Spring Creek.
Photo by Brian Grossenbacher.

Table of Contents

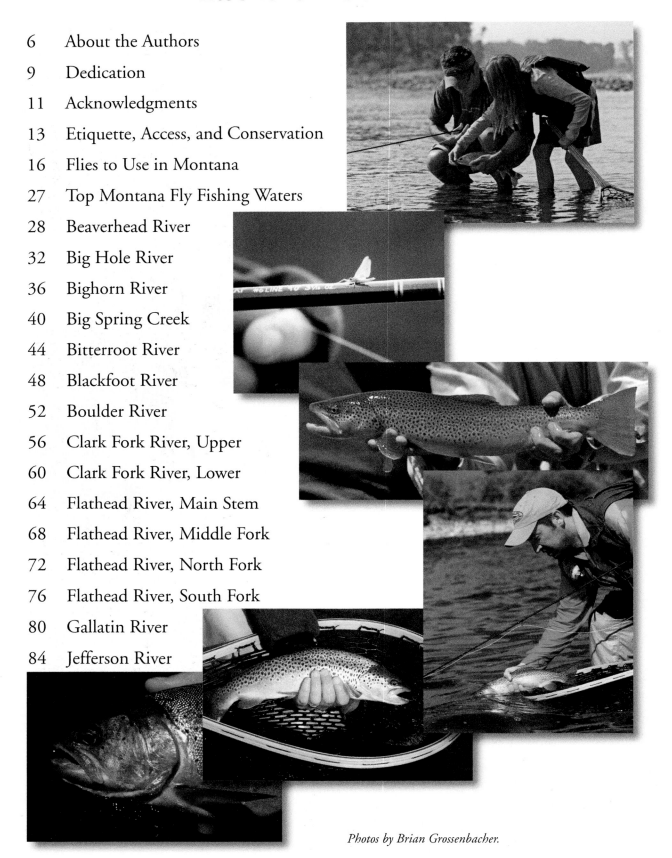

Photos by Brian Grossenbacher.

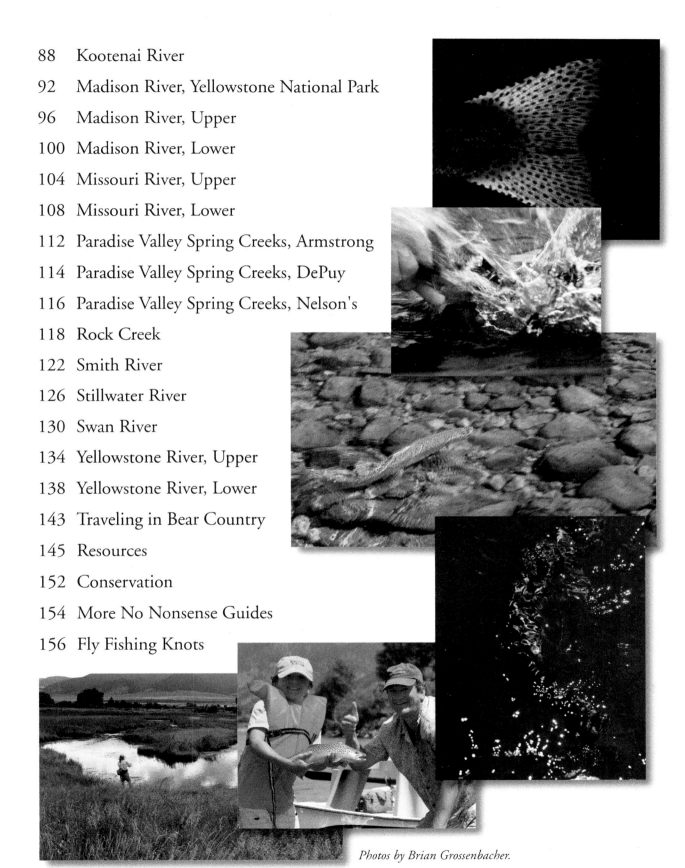

Photos by Brian Grossenbacher.

5

Brian Grossenbacher. Photo by Andy Anderson.

About the Author

In German, Grossenbacher literally translates to Big River and according to some accounts, Keeper of the Brook, both translations of which the Grossenbachers have taken to heart. Surrounded by more than 800 miles of blue ribbon trout water, the Grossenbachers' home waters include the Madison, Yellowstone, and Gallatin Rivers along with the famous Paradise Valley spring creeks.

Brian Grossenbacher has a BA from Wabash College and a Masters in Education from Montana State University. Brian grew up fishing for pike, walleye, and bass with his father and grandfather but turned to the art of flyfishing after much prodding from his college buddy Mark Scott. Brian is the author of the Tying Flies Workstation, a comprehensive beginner's guide to tying flies, which has sold over 60,000 copies worldwide. He has also published articles in *Fly Fisherman, Saltwater Fly Fishing, Flyfishing Quarterly* and *River* magazines. Brian's photography has also been featured in *The Drake, Fly Fisherman, Field & Stream, Fly Rod & Reel, Fly Fish America, Saltwater Fly Fishing, Trout,* and the *Trout Unlimited Calendar* as well as various Orvis catalogs.

Brian was honored in the 2006 issue of *The Drake* featured with six other fly fishing photographers revealing their favorite photos.

Jenny Grossenbacher. Photo by Brian Grossenbacher.

About the Author

Jenny Grossenbacher has a BA in philosophy and a BS in Fish Wildlife Biology. While working as a backpacking guide in New Mexico in 1988 she met Brian, also a guide. After a youth of worm fishing on White Rock Lake in Dallas, Brian led Jenny to take up the higher pursuits of fly fishing. She has avidly fished and explored the Rocky Mountains ever since.

In addition to guiding fly fishing trips for more than 13 years, Jenny has led grizzly bear research projects in both Yellowstone and Glacier National Parks, and songbird studies throughout Southwest Montana.

She has appeared as guest host on Flyfishing America, and Gray's Sporting Journal Television. Jenny was also selected as one of twelve international anglers to participate in ESPN's 2001 Great Outdoor Games in Lake Placid, New York where she competed with some of the best anglers in the world including casting champions from three countries. In 2002 Jenny competed and placed 2nd in ESPN's 2002 Rocky Mountain Team Flyfishing Championships where she was an integral part of Team Sage.

Jenny has published articles and been featured in an assortment of publications including *American Angler, Big Sky Journal, Gray's Sporting Journal, Saltwater Sportsman, Women & Fitness, Sporting Classics, Northwest Flyfishing, Saltwater Fly Fishing, Rocky Mountain Game & Fish, Wild On The Fly,* and *Outdoor America* magazines. She has also appeared in several outdoor calendars as well as in the LL Bean, Dan Bailey, The Fly Shop, and Simms product catalogs. She has served as a board member for the Federation of Fly Fishers, Headwaters Chapter.

Jenny and Brian have two daughters, Mackenzie and Sable as well as four Labrador Retrievers, including two rescued from the Yellowstone River. They have called Montana home for more than 17 years.

Ty Elliot hooked up near Bozeman, Montana.
Photo by Brian Grossenbacher.

Dedication

This guide is dedicated to our daughters, Mackenzie and Sable,
who endlessly question when it is their turn to fish with us.
May you always yearn to join us and may we always make the
time to include you.
To Jenny's brother Robert who led her down the path to the
Rocky Mountains and eventually to Brian and flyfishing.
To Mark Scott, Brian's college buddy who introduced him to
the passion of flyfishing in an attempt to survive college.
And of course to our parents, Robert and Lloyd-Ann
McMahan, and John and Judy Grossenbacher, who without
their continual support and patience, as well as their loving
care for our daughters, we would find difficulty in pursuing
what we love to do…

Sable and Mackenzie Grossenbacher.
Photo by Brian Grossenbacher.

Fall in Montana without another angler in sight.
Photo by Brian Grossenbacher.

Acknowledgments

Although Jenny and I have fished all over the state, our home waters lie in southwest Montana. For many of the rivers outside of our region we drew upon the expertise of local guides, outfitters, fly shop owners and managers who spend their lives fishing on those waters. Very special thanks go out to Evan Phillippe from the Grizzly Hackle for his assistance of the vast and productive fisheries in and around the Missoula area. We would also like to thank Tim and Joanne Linehan of Linehan Outfitting Company for their help on the Kootenai River and other Northwestern Montana waters. Thanks also go out to Jason Wise, a veteran Bighorn guide turned urban professional who drew upon his many days on the Bighorn to help us out. We cannot offer enough thanks to our guide staff who have helped build our business into what it is today through their commitment to the sport of fly fishing and by investing one hundred percent of their efforts into the success of our business. Special thanks should also be given to all clients, fishing buddies, and guides who repeatedly allowed us to photograph them for this book:

Cale VanVelkinburgh	Don Anderson	Doug Nail
Casey Dudley	Jeff Spahr	Jerry Fitzsimmons
Charles Johnson	Chip and Julia Kern	Jimmy Kloote
Chuck Borg	John Walker	Liz and Jim Morgan
Craig Boyd	Tom Fournie	Tom Stover
Ty Elliot		

And to anyone else who we photographed, but whose picture ended up on the editing room floor.

We would also like to thank Steve, Dan and the crew at the River's Edge Fly Shop in Bozeman for welcoming our clients for more than a decade.

Finally, we would like to thank our publisher, Howard Fisher for selecting us to do this project and to Morenci Clark and Pete Chadwell for their work in the design and layout of this book.

Mid-summer on the Yellowstone.
Photo by Brian Grossenbacher.

The Big Hole Valley and surrounding tributaries provide some of the most remarkable landscapes in Montana. Photo by Brian Grossenbacher

Etiquette, Access, and Conservation

There is no shortage of water to fish in Montana, which may not seem to be the case when you arrive at a boat ramp early and there is a line of trucks, boats and trailers waiting to get into the water. The solution is simple—spread out. If you pull into a crowded boat ramp or access point, continue on up or downstream until you find a less crowded one. Doing so reduces the pressure and crowding, greatly enhancing your fishing experience. Spreading out doesn't have to mean leaving your favorite water altogether, but rather spreading out on the clock by putting in early in the morning or later in the afternoon. It could mean planning a mid-week trip on popular waters rather than a weekend excursion. It could mean planning your trips during the shoulder seasons—March, April, October, or November. In fact, our best fish of the year are frequently caught during these months as the fish are either bulking up after a long cold winter or preparing for the upcoming one. It could mean hiking in a few miles rather than fishing within sight of an access site. You would be surprised how many people drive or fly hundreds—even thousands of miles—to get to Montana then never get out of sight of the first bridge that gives them access to the water. The journey doesn't end when you hit the water—it has only just begun. Explore the smaller streams that feed the major rivers. Get off the beaten path and hike into a mountain lake. Be the first to discover the next secret fishing hole.

Wade Fishing

Interaction with other anglers is a way of life on popular waters. Communicate with fellow anglers to let them know your intentions and to find out theirs. Give them a wide berth on the streams—your presence should never negatively affect their fishing or experience. If you are rigging up at the same time on a small stream, plot a game plan—one person goes upstream and the other goes down. If you see an angler fishing a favorite hole of yours, don't sit and wait him out. Instead, move on to find new water. Likewise, do not stay in one spot and monopolize the good fishing. Catch a few and move on. When approaching other anglers, use care not to spook fish they may be casting to. Avoid crossing immediately upstream of other anglers, or walking too close to an overhanging bank they may be fishing. There are really no cut and dried answers to how close is too close. The general rule is the fewer the people, the more you should spread out. Respect others and enjoy the serenity the sport offers.

Fishing From a Boat or Personal Water Craft

If you float Montana waters bear in mind a few simple rules:

At the ramp:
- Wait your turn before approaching the boat ramp.
- Do not block the boat ramp by rigging your craft while on the ramp. Have your boat and gear ready to go before you approach the ramp. Launch your boat quickly and clear the ramp for other users.
- Anchor your boat in a secure location clear of the ramp while you park your vehicle.
- At the end of the day prepare your boat for trailering before you back down the ramp. Once you back down the ramp, load your boat quickly onto the trailer and clear the ramp. Do not strap down or unload your boat until you clear the ramp area. All boat ramps have substantial parking areas where you can secure your boat and gear without blocking the ramp.

On the water:
- Always look upstream before you pull anchor and head into the current. Moving boats have the right of way (do not pull out in front of approaching craft). Remember, the fewer the people on the water, the more you should spread out.
- Wading anglers have the right of way. Give them plenty of room, and avoid the water they are fishing. If in doubt, communicate. There may be instances where the wading angler should yield to floaters if there is no other channel for the floater to navigate.
- If you overtake another boat, give them plenty of room before you pull back into their lane.
- Treat anchored boats the same as wading anglers. Even if they are not fishing, they may be spotting rising fish—give them plenty of room, and respect their space.
- Never drag an anchor to control or slow your floating craft. Pull to the side of the river out of the current and then drop anchor to stop the craft completely.

Catch and release fishing can enhance the experience of fishing for generations to come. Photo by Brian Grossenbacher.

Most fishing access sites require you to pack in and pack out garbage. Please do not discard garbage in the outhouses.

Conservation

With more fly fishermen entering the sport each season we should take great care to preserve our fisheries and aquatic ecosystems every step of the way. Catch and release fishermen should always use barbless hooks, and play and release fish quickly. Wet your hands before handling fish to eliminate damage to their protective slime layer or better yet release the fish without touching them. Use forceps or another releasing tool instead, such as the Ketchum Release (available at most fly shops). With practice you will wonder how you ever released fish without one. See www.waterworks-lamson.com/ketchum.html.

If you wish to take a photo of the fish, keep the camera in a readily accessible location, and make sure your fishing partner is familiar with your camera. Keep the fish in the water until you are ready to snap the photo. Try to position the fish low to the water so that if it slips from your grasp it will not become injured. Never squeeze a fish. It will simply slip from your hands like a wet bar of soap and, most importantly, may sustain terminal internal bruising.

Release a fish facing upstream in clean, oxygenated water. Let the fish swim away from you under its own power. It is not necessary to move the fish back and forth in the current to oxygenate its gills, allow the moving water do that for you.

As a wading angler, stay on the stream banks whenever possible to prevent damage to aquatic habitat. It is not just the fish that we need to preserve, but the valuable and fragile aquatic ecosystem.

Rights and Responsibilities of Landowners and Recreationists

The following information has been taken directly from the Montana Fish Wildlife and Parks website and summarizes the ways in which Montana's 1985 stream access law affects the recreational use of the state's rivers and streams and incorporates the ways the law has been interpreted by the courts in Montana.

The law states that rivers and streams capable of recreational use may be so used by the public regardless of streambed ownership. It also states that certain activities require landowner permission. Because the law affects your rights and responsibilities as a landowner or recreationist, the information that follows may be of interest to you.

Trespass Legislation

This legislation states that a member of the public has the privilege to enter or remain on private land by the explicit permission of the landowner or his agent or by the failure of the landowner to post notice denying entry onto the land. The landowner may revoke the permission by personal communication. (For more detail see H.B. 911 from the 1985 session.)

The law states that notice denying entry must consist of written notice or of notice by painting a post, structure or natural object with at least 50 square inches of fluorescent orange paint. In the case of a metal fencepost, the entire post must be painted. This notice must be placed at each outer gate and all normal points of access to the property and wherever a stream crosses an outer boundary line.

The law also extends the authority of game wardens to enforce the criminal mischief, criminal trespass and litter laws to all lands being used by the public for recreational purposes.

Montana Stream Access Law

Under the Montana Stream Access Law, the public may use rivers and streams for recreational purposes up to the ordinary high-water marks. Although the law gives recreationists the right to use rivers and streams for water-related recreation, it does not allow them to enter posted lands bordering those streams or to cross private lands to gain access to streams. Complete rules are available at any Montana Fish Wildlife and Parks office.

National Parks, Indian Reservations, and Wildlife Refuges

Certain waters on national parks, Indian reservations and wildlife refuges may have special rules. Specific information may be obtained from the headquarters of the park, reservation, or refuge involved.

For further information concerning access laws, please contact the Department's Conservation Education Division in Helena at (406) 444-2535, or one of the Department's regional offices.

Copies of the law may be obtained by sending a request to the Montana Legislative Council, Room 138, Capitol Building, Helena, MT 59620, or by calling (406) 444-3064.

The fish gods smile on law-abiding anglers. Photo by Brian Grossenbacher.

Flies to Use in Montana–Drys

Adult Midge

Blue Winged Olive

Blue Winged Olive Cripple

Bullet Golden Stone

Bullet Head Skwala

BWO Biot

BWO Comparadun

Callibeatis Cripple

Carlson's Purple Haze Parachute

Carnage Stone Skwala

CDC Comparadun Baetis

CDC Green Drake Parachute

CDC Sparkle Dun

Comparadun

Black Caddis

E/C Caddis

Elk Caddis

Goddard Caddis

Grifffith's Gnat

GT BWO

GT Mahogany

Harrop's CDC Cripple BWO

Hot Butt Caddis

Light Cahill

Light Hendrickson

Midge Cluster

Missoula Skwala

Pale Morning Dun

Pale Morning Dun Cripple

Parachute Hare's Ear Olive

Parachute Adams

Parachute Light Cahill

Parachute Trico

Paralyzer Golden Stone

Quill Gordon

Red Quill

Rogue Stone

Royal Stimulator

RS2 Emerger

Rusty Spinner

Sofa Pillow

Trico Sparkle Dun

Stimulator

Trico

X Caddis

Yellow Sally

Yellow Stimulator

Triple Wing Spinner

Flies to Use–Terrestrials & Attractors

Black Fur Ant

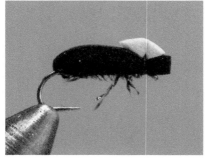

Beetle

Flying Ant

Bugmeister

Cherry Chernobyl

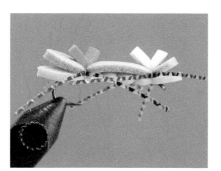

Chernobyl Hopper

Convertible

Dave's Hopper

Hoppinator

Humpy

Lime Trude

Madam X

Parachute Hopper

PMX

Rainy's Grand Hopper

Renegade

Rogue Hopper

Royal Trude

Royal Wulff

Speckled X

Steeves' Crystal Butt Hopper

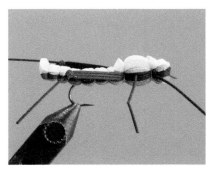

Tripledecker

Turk's Tarantula

Whit's Hopper

Flies to Use–Large Nymphs/Streamers

Anderson's Brown Stone

Bitch Creek Nymph

Black Rubber Legs

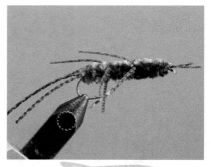

Brown Rubber Legs

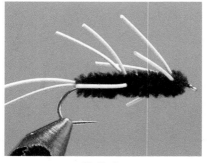

Girdle Bug

Kaufmann's Stone

Mega Prince

Poxyback Stone Nymph

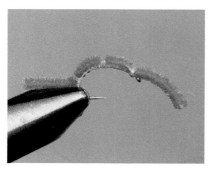

San Juan Worm

Speckled Double Beaded Stone

Twenty Incher

Crystal Bugger

Bow River Bugger

Clouser Crayfish

Clouser Minnow Deep

Conehead Bugger

Double Bunny

Olive Bugger

J.J. Special

McCune's™ Sculpin

Muddler Minnow

Whitlock's Crayfish

Zirdle Bug

Copper Zonker

Flies to Use–Small Nymphs

Barr's Emerger

Flashback Bead Head Hare's Ear Nymph

Bead Head Pheasant Tail Nymph

Bead Head Prince Nymph

Bead Head Zebra Midge

BLM, Red

Brassie

Bubble Back Pheasant Tail

Copper John

Dave's Emerger

Diamond Soft Hackle

Disco Midge

Flashback Pheasant Tail

Lightning Bug

Olive Serendipity

Lime Green Midge

Palomino Midge

Prince

Sawyer's Pheasant Tail

Scud

Sparkle Pupa

Yellow Prince

WD-40

Yellow Sally Nymph

Float fishing is arguably the most enjoyable way to experience the Yellowstone.
Photo by Brian Grossenbacher.

Top Montana Fly Fishing Waters

Photos by Brian Grossenbacher.

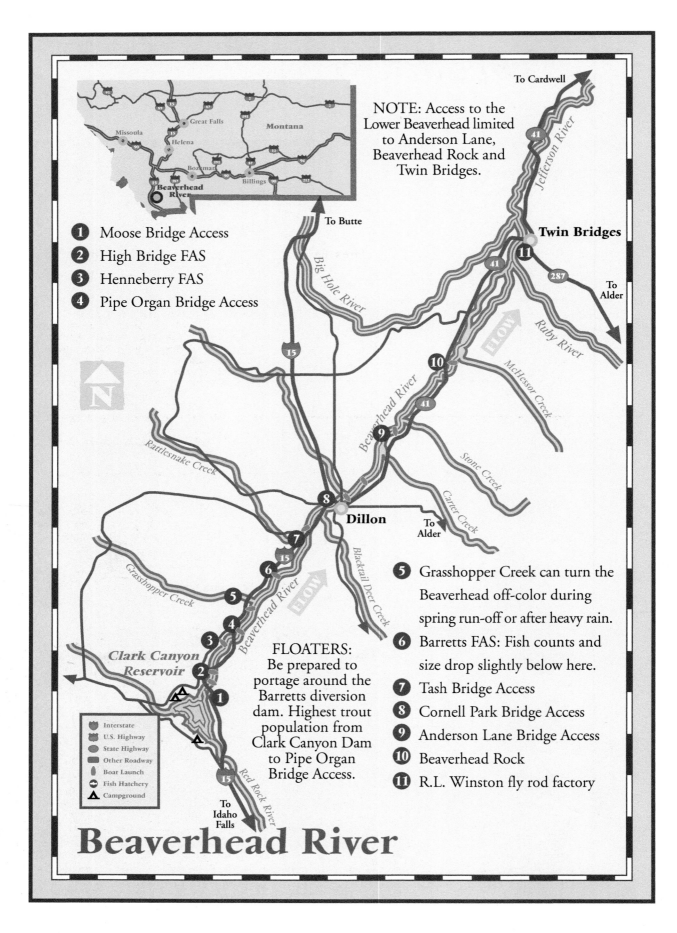

NOTE: Access to the Lower Beaverhead limited to Anderson Lane, Beaverhead Rock and Twin Bridges.

1 Moose Bridge Access
2 High Bridge FAS
3 Henneberry FAS
4 Pipe Organ Bridge Access

FLOATERS:
Be prepared to portage around the Barretts diversion dam. Highest trout population from Clark Canyon Dam to Pipe Organ Bridge Access.

5 Grasshopper Creek can turn the Beaverhead off-color during spring run-off or after heavy rain.
6 Barretts FAS: Fish counts and size drop slightly below here.
7 Tash Bridge Access
8 Cornell Park Bridge Access
9 Anderson Lane Bridge Access
10 Beaverhead Rock
11 R.L. Winston fly rod factory

Interstate
U.S. Highway
State Highway
Other Roadway
Boat Launch
Fish Hatchery
Campground

Beaverhead River

Beaverhead River

If you believe that good things come in small packages, then you will certainly find a gem in the Beaverhead River. The Beaverhead originates below the Clark Canyon reservoir and twists and turns for more than 80 miles until it merges with the Ruby and then the Big Hole River to form the Jefferson. Although small in stature, the Beaverhead is not lacking for large trout, and in fact has built a reputation as a trophy brown trout fishery. The Beaverhead has good dry fly fishing, but it is primarily a small nymph river.

Popular patterns include Pheasant Tails, Hare's Ears, Serendipities, Brassies, Miracle Nymphs and Copper Johns all in the #16-20 range. The brushy banks and deep pools of the Beaverhead favor the float fishermen throughout all but the lowest flows (below 300 CFS).

The Beaverhead is one of the busiest rivers in Montana and crowding is a concern at peak season. Restrictions have been placed on the river, both for guides and out-of-state anglers. Check in at one of the local fly shops or the Fish Wildlife and Parks (406) 994-4042 for updated restrictions. To avoid crowding, consider that 90% of guides meet their clients at 8:00 am and fish until 5:00 or 6:00 pm. Time your fishing to put in ahead of the guides or after. One of the most memorable days of flyfishing in Montana occurred when Jenny and I put in at Henneberry at 2:30 on a late July afternoon, and fished until

Types of Fish:
Brown and Rainbow Trout, Whitefish.

Known Hatches:
Early April-Early June: Baetis.
May-September: Caddis.
Late June-July: Yellow Sallies.
Late June-Early August: Pale Morning Duns (PMDs), Hoppers.
August-September: Tricos, Spruce Moths, Craneflies.
Late September-October: Baetis.

Equipment to Use:
Rods: 5-6 weight, 8½-9 feet in length.
Lines: Floating line.
Leaders: 9-12' 4-6x for dry, 7½-9' 3-4x for nymphs, 7½' 0-2x fluorocarbon for streamers.
Wading: Difficult except at low water, brushy banks.

Flies to Use:
Dries: Griffith's Gnat #18-22, CDC Olive Emerger #18-22, Elk Hair Caddis #12-18, Goddard Caddis #10-16, Parachute Adams #16-20, Royal Wulff #10-16, PMX #8-14, Ants #12-20, Beetles #14-18, Parachute Trico #20-24, Stimulator #14-18, Hoppers #6-12, Turk's Tarantula #8-12, Darbee Cranefly #8-14.
Nymphs: Pheasant Tail #14-20, Brassie #18-22, Serendipity #16-22, Lightning Bugs #16-18, Copper Johns #12-18, Hare's Ears #12-18, Sparkle Pupa #12-20, San Juan Worms, Wet Ants #12-18, Cranefly larvae #8-12.
Streamers: Woolly Bugger, JJ Special, Muddler & Clouser Minnow.

Jenny Grossenbacher and Maddie on the Upper Beaverhead.
Photo by Brian Grossenbacher.

A nice brown ready for release.
Photo by Brian Grossenbacher.

dark. By that time we were behind all of the other boats and enjoyed the evening caddis hatch to ourselves.

The Beaverhead is commonly divided into 3 sections. The first section from Clark Canyon to Barretts Dam has the greatest concentration of large fish and, unfortunately, fishermen. These fish are cagey veterans and require accurate, drag-free presentations, and delicate tippet. Be prepared to lose plenty of flies both to the fish and the heavy brush thoroughly lining the twisting banks of the Beaverhead. Access is easily gained via multiple exits off Highway 15 South from Dillon.

The second section is from Barretts Dam to Dillon. The fish counts drop in this section and, not surprisingly, so do angler numbers. As a result the fish are not as particular and larger flies and heavier tippets can be used. Due to the large volume of water diverted at Barretts, mid-summer flows can be a problem for floaters. Access is limited to Barretts, Tash Bridge, and Cornell Park via access road 222 out of Dillon. However, there are still decent numbers of large fish in this section and because they are not as picky, your success may be similar to fishing the upper section.

The lower third of the Beaverhead broadens and slows as the river approaches Twin Bridges. The river flows through open farmland, and the temperatures increase in the late summer months. Access is again limited, but this seclusion can offer opportunities to enjoy a less-populated Beaverhead. Due to the fluctuations in temperature, fishing in this stretch is most productive in the spring, early summer and fall. Access at Anderson Lane Bridge, Beaverhead Rock and Twin Bridges are clearly marked and accessible off Highway 41 between Twin Bridges and Dillon.

Regardless of the stretch you choose, the Beaverhead is a demanding float in which the oarsman must continually battle tight turns, swift currents, irrigation diversions, and the occasional fence across the river.

The Clark Canyon Reservoir supplies large browns and rainbows for the Beaverhead. Photo by Brian Grossenbacher.

When to Fish:

From opening day on the third Saturday in May throughout the summer the Beaverhead fishes well, especially up higher where the water temperatures are kept cool by the Clark Canyon Reservoir. By the time mid July rolls around the crowding is not as big of an issue. The warmer temperatures and lower flows of late summer slow down the fishing, however it picks up again in fall with the movement of the big browns.

Seasons & Limits:

The standard fishing regulations for the *Central* fishing district apply. Please check the *Montana Fishing Regulations and Etiquette* section.

Exceptions to Standard Regulations

Clark Canyon Dam to Anderson Lane
Combined Trout: 3 daily and in possession, only 1 over 18 inches and only 1 rainbow trout.

Clark Canyon Dam to Pipe Organ Bridge
Open third Saturday in May through November 30.

High Bridge FAS to Henneberry FAS
Closed to float fishing by nonresidents and float outfitting on each Saturday from the third Saturday in May through Labor Day.

Henneberry FAS to Pipe Organ Bridge
Closed to float fishing by nonresidents and float outfitting on each Sunday from the third Sunday in May through Labor Day.

Downstream from Pipe Organ Bridge
Open entire year.

Highway 91 South Bridge (Tash Bridge) to Selway Bridge
Closed to float outfitting from the third Saturday in May through Labor Day.

Anderson Lane Downstream to Mouth (Near Twin Bridges)
Combined Trout: 5 daily and in possession, 1 over 18 inches, only 1 may be a rainbow trout.

Nearby Fly Fishing:

Clark Canyon Reservoir, Poindexter Slough, Big Hole River, and Ruby River.

Accommodations & Services:

Dillon is about 20 miles downstream from the best section of fishing. There are many lodges and rental cabins in Dillon, including Tom Smith's Backcountry Angler (406-683-3402, www.backcountryangler.com), where you can also find a fly shop. The best camping is arguably at Clark Canyon Reservoir.

Rating: 8

The top 10 miles of the Beaverhead down from the Clark Canyon Reservoir rank a solid 9 due to the trophy trout to be found. Below the first stretch mentioned above, the fishing tapers off significantly, warranting only a 7 for a rating. All said, the Beaverhead offers a classic tailwater fishing experience surrounded by other excellent fishing opportunities.

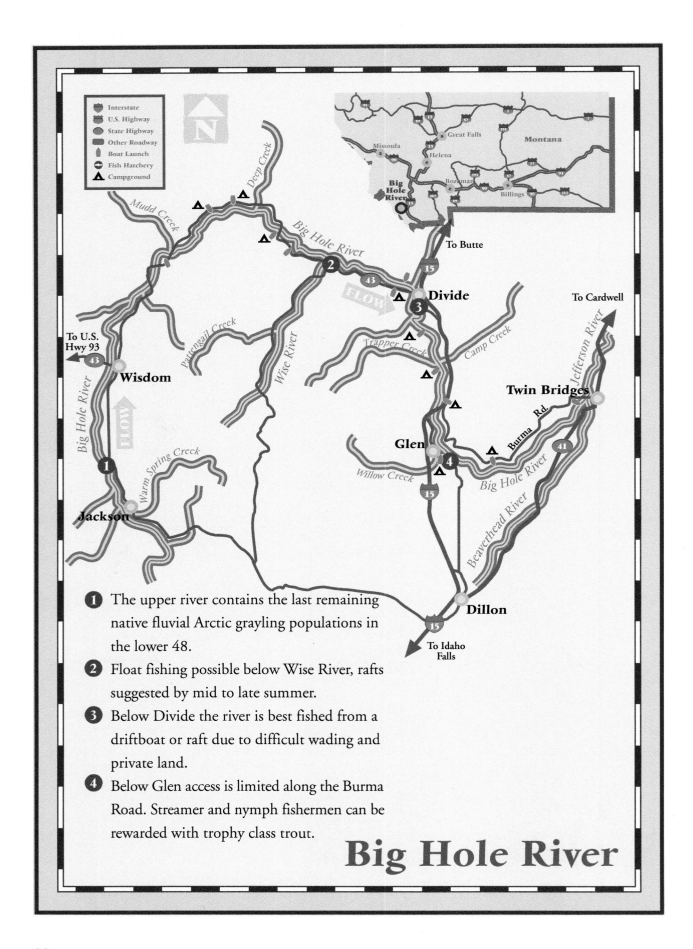

Legend:
- Interstate
- U.S. Highway
- State Highway
- Other Roadway
- Boat Launch
- Fish Hatchery
- Campground

N

Montana

Missoula
Great Falls
Helena
Bozeman
Billings
Big Hole River

Deep Creek

Mudd Creek

Big Hole River

To Butte

Divide

Pattengail Creek

Wise River

Trapper Creek

Camp Creek

Jefferson River

To Cardwell

To U.S. Hwy 93

Wisdom

Twin Bridges

Burma Rd.

Big Hole River

FLOW

Warm Spring Creek

Glen

Willow Creek

Beaverhead River

Jackson

Dillon

To Idaho Falls

1 The upper river contains the last remaining native fluvial Arctic grayling populations in the lower 48.

2 Float fishing possible below Wise River, rafts suggested by mid to late summer.

3 Below Divide the river is best fished from a driftboat or raft due to difficult wading and private land.

4 Below Glen access is limited along the Burma Road. Streamer and nymph fishermen can be rewarded with trophy class trout.

Big Hole River

Big Hole River

Lewis and Clark referred to it as the "Wisdom," but the name "Big Hole," coined by early trappers and settlers in reference to the high elevation valley through which the river flows, stuck, and that is how we have come to know one of the most beautiful trout streams in the state of Montana. The Big Hole flows freely without dams for 115 miles to its confluence with the Beaverhead, and eventually the Ruby, to form the Jefferson around mile 153. The Big Hole begins its serpentine course across western Montana high in the Beaverhead Mountains at Skinner Lake. The upper section of the Big Hole is easily wadeable with several access points at county road crossings and federal and state maintained fishing access sites. From Jackson to the town of Wisdom, the river braids and turns through rich pasture land, and thick willow banks. Downstream from Wisdom, the river opens generously, inviting both the wading angler as well as float fisherman. The upper section of the Big Hole hosts cutthroat, rainbow, brook trout and most notably, is home to the last remaining native population of fluvial (river dwelling) Arctic grayling in the lower 48.

Throughout its course, the Big Hole is steadily enhanced from feeder streams and at the junction of Wise River matures into a large trout river. Drift boat fishing is possible through early summer, though rafts are suggested by mid to late summer. Arguably, the best fishing on the Big Hole is found from Wise River to Glen. However, no one will dispute that this section also receives the most attention from anglers. Downstream from

The upper Big Hole is home to the last remaining native population of fluvial Arctic grayling in the lower 48. Photo by Brian Grossenbacher.

Types of Fish:
Rainbow, Brown, Brook and Cutthroat Trout, Arctic Grayling, Whitefish.

Known Hatches:
Late March-Mid April: Skwala Stones.
Late April-Early May: Caddis.
Mid May-July: Golden Stones.
Mid June-Mid July: Salmonflies.
June-July: Green & Brown Drakes.
July: Yellow Sallies.
July-Early August: Pale Morning Duns (PMDs).
August-September: Tricos, Spruce Moths.

Equipment to Use:
Rods: 5-6 weight, 9 feet in length.
Lines: Floating line, sink tip for streamer fishing deep.
Leaders: 7½' 2-3x for nymphing, 9' 4-6x for dries, 7½' 0-2x fluorocarbon for streamers.
Wading: Waist-high waders are fine most of the year.

Flies to Use:
Dries: Royal Wulff #12-16, PMX #8-12, Parachute Adams #10-18, Stimulator #10-16, Ants #18-20, Elk Hair Caddis #14-18.
Nymphs: Bullethead Skwala #8-10, Olive Stonefly #8-10, Poxyback Stone Nymph #6-10, Brown Rubber Legs #6-10, Kaufmann's Gold Stone #6-10, Bitch Creek #4-6, Rogue Stones #4-8, Rubber Legs #4-6, Kaufmann's Stone #4-6, Hare's Ear Nymph #10-18, Pheasant Tail Nymph #10-16, Trico nymph #18-22, Copper John #10-16, Beadhead or plain Prince Nymph #12-16, Lightning Bug #12-18, San Juan Worm.
Streamers: Olive Bugger #2-6, Leech #2-8, JJ Special #2-6, Muddler & Clouser Minnow #2-6.

When to Fish:
The Big Hole River is famous for its Salmonfly hatch which frequently is at its height between mid June and early July. Although some people are concerned with the low water conditions that can be found in late summer, big fish can be caught on tricos and spruce moths in August. Due to the surrounding hay fields, count on great hopper fishing in late July and early August. Add good streamer fishing in early and late season and you can stretch out the season as far as you'd like.

Seasons & Limits:
Standard fishing regulations for the *Central* fishing district apply. Please check the *Montana Fishing Regulations and Etiquette* section. The Big Hole River has multiple exceptions and restrictions so check below carefully or check in with FWP.
Exceptions to Standard Regulations
Entire River and Tributaries
Catch-and-release for grayling and cutthroat trout. All float users are limited to a total of 2 launches at or near each official access site each day. See Big Hole River map for official access sites. Extended season for whitefish and catch-and-release for trout open December 1 to the third Saturday in May with artificial lures and/or maggots only.

The Big Hole flows through some of the most spectacular scenery Montana has to offer. Photo by Brian Grossenbacher.

Wise River the Big Hole bounds over boulders and thunders through tight canyon walls from Dewey to Maiden Rock and it gradually opens again into broad pasture land around Melrose. This middle section is primarily a brown trout fishery with smaller numbers of rainbows. Access is plentiful via Highway 43 to Divide, and from the frontage road off I-15 between Divide and Glen. Below Divide the river is best fished from a drift boat or raft due to its difficult wading, shallow boulders, and isolated corridor through private land.

The final section of the Big Hole, from Glen to the confluence of the Beaverhead, parts ways with Interstate 15 and journeys off the beaten path. The river opens and slows as it makes its final northeast turn. This section is also best fished from a boat or raft as access is limited to Glen, Notch Bottom, Pennington Bridge, and High Road, all along Burma Road on the route to Twin Bridges. Although the fish count drops, the float down to Pennington Bridge is another guide favorite due to the trophy browns awaiting the patient angler, especially those fishing large nymphs and streamers. While the neighboring Beaverhead River is famous for its trophy trout, local guides often claim that year after year they take their largest fish of the summer out of the Big Hole.

Even though the Big Hole flows through sparsely-populated ranch land, it is one of the heavier fished rivers in the state, and has recently received experimental regulations governing outfitters and out-of-state anglers. The regulations are at best controversial and have many an outfitter up in arms. The regulations restrict non-resident and commercial use float fishing to six days a week, with one stretch of river out of seven closed each day. Wade fishing is still allowed on these days. To ensure you follow the rules, contact http://fwp.state.mt.us/fishing/regulations or call (406) 994-4042.

Another nice Big Hole brown.
Photo by Brian Grossenbacher.

Headwaters to Mudd Creek FAS
   Closed to float outfitting from the third Saturday in May through Labor Day.
Mudd Creek FAS to Fishtrap FAS
   Closed to float outfitting on each Tuesday from the third Saturday in May through Labor Day.
Fishtrap FAS to East Bank BLM FAS
   Closed to float outfitting on each Thursday from the third Saturday in May through Labor Day.
East Bank BLM FAS to Jerry Creek FAS
   Closed to float outfitting on each Wednesday from the third Saturday in May through Labor Day.
Tributaries Upstream from Divide Dam
   Brook trout: open entire year.
Dickie Bridge to Divide Bridge (Divide FAS)
   Artificial lures only.
Jerry Creek FAS to Divide FAS
   Closed to float fishing by nonresidents and float outfitting on each Saturday from the third Saturday in May through Labor Day.
Divide Bridge (Divide FAS) to Melrose Bridges (Salmon Fly FAS)
   Combined Trout: 4 daily and in possession, includes 3 under 13 inches and 1 over 22 inches.
   Artificial lures only.
   Closed to float fishing by nonresidents and float outfitting on each Sunday from the third Saturday in May through Labor Day.
Melrose Bridges (Salmon Fly FAS) to Glen FAS (Bridges)
   Closed to float outfitting on each Monday from the third Saturday in May through Labor Day.
Glen FAS (Bridges) to Notch Bottom FAS
   Closed to float outfitting on each Friday from the third Saturday in May through Labor Day.

Nearby Fly Fishing:
Beaverhead, Ruby, Pointdexter Slough, Clark Canyon Reservoir.

Accommodations & Services:
There are campsites at Forest Service campgrounds, including Twin Lakes, Van Houten, Bannack State Park, East Bank, and Dickie Bridge. As for lodging, be ready to drive a little in one direction or the other. The Nez Perce Hotel (406-689-3254) in Wisdom is the only thing around in the upper stretches while the Sportsman's (406-835-2141) gets the job done if you are closer to Melrose. Dillon offers a vast array of lodges and rental cabins including Tom Smith's Backcountry Angler (406-683-3402: www.backcountryangler.com) which also offers a flyshop. Another excellent option in Wise River is Craig Fellin Outfitters and Big Hole Lodge (406-832-3252: www.flyfishinglodge.com).

Rating: 9
The beauty of the Big Hole and the majesty of the surrounding mountains is worth its weight in gold. Add in great fishing, proximity to an assortment of other blue ribbon trout streams plus a historical trip to the Big Hole Battlefield, and you have a home run of a river. A strong 9, with the limiting factor being the dewatering of the river for agricultural purposes in late summer.

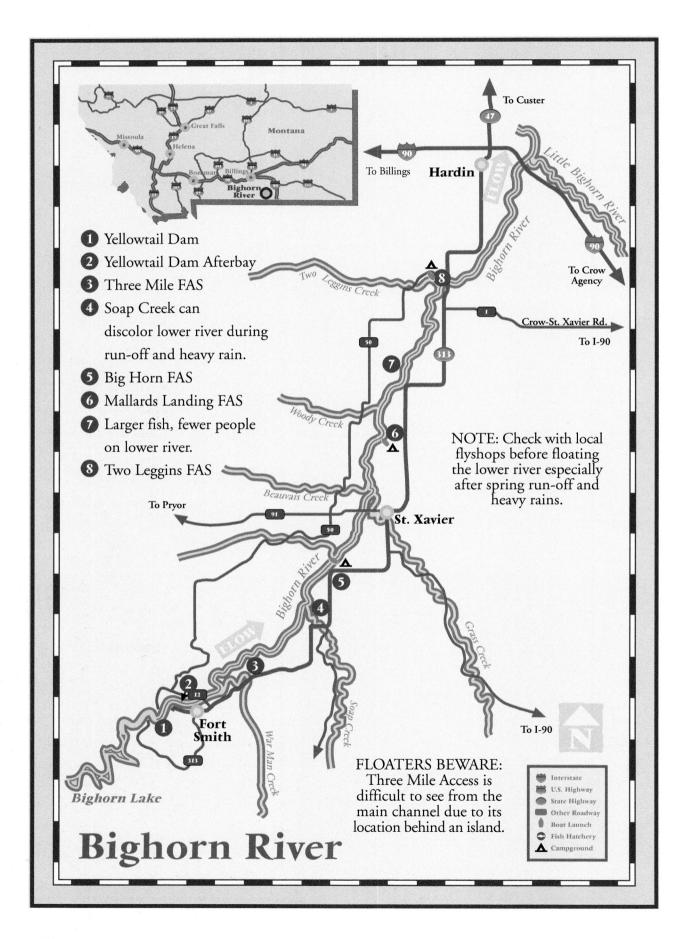

1 Yellowtail Dam

2 Yellowtail Dam Afterbay

3 Three Mile FAS

4 Soap Creek can discolor lower river during run-off and heavy rain.

5 Big Horn FAS

6 Mallards Landing FAS

7 Larger fish, fewer people on lower river.

8 Two Leggins FAS

NOTE: Check with local flyshops before floating the lower river especially after spring run-off and heavy rains.

FLOATERS BEWARE: Three Mile Access is difficult to see from the main channel due to its location behind an island.

Interstate
U.S. Highway
State Highway
Other Roadway
Boat Launch
Fish Hatchery
Campground

Bighorn River

Bighorn River

The Bighorn River is 112 miles in length; however, most anglers find interest in the 13-mile stretch below the Afterbay Dam (just a few miles downstream from the Yellowtail Dam) at the town of Fort Smith. Prior to 1965, the Bighorn River was warm, silty, and of little interest to trout fishermen. The completion of the Yellowtail dam, and subsequently the Afterbay dam in 1967, changed the character of the Bighorn virtually overnight by allowing the silt to settle and the water to cool in the deep water of the newly-constructed Bighorn reservoir. The portion of the river that flows through Crow Indian territory was closed to the general public in 1975. It was re-opened following a heated Supreme Court ruling that declared the river public in 1981. Public access is now available at three points on the upper 13 miles of river: Afterbay, 3 Mile (Lind Ranch) and 13 Mile (Big Horn Access).

Although the Big Horn River is a relative newcomer to the sport of flyfishing, it has comfortably settled into its role as a powerhouse tailwater trout factory. The recipe for success begins with the relative alkalinity of the water. The nutrient-rich ph borne from the limestone walls of the Bighorn Canyon creates a perfect environment for the aquatic insect population, and as go the bugs, so go the trout. Add a healthy supply of cool, clear, water and it is easy to see why the Bighorn has at times hosted up to 10,000 trout per mile, with an average size of 16"-18", in its relative short history. That being said, the Bighorn is currently enduring tough times as a result of multiple drought years in Eastern Montana. Although fish counts are down, size classes are up, and anglers still have plenty to smile about in Fort Smith.

Types of Fish:
Brown and Rainbow Trout, Whitefish.

Known Hatches:
Year-round: Midges, Scuds, Sowbugs, Streamers, Craneflies, Leeches.
Mid March-Late April: Baetis.
Late April-Mid July: Caddis, Baetis.
Mid June-July: PMDs, Caddis, Ants, Beetles, Tricos, Baetis, Yellow Sallies.
August-October: Black Caddis, Hoppers, Tricos, Baetis, Streamers.

Equipment to Use:
Rods: 5-7 weight, 8½-9 feet in length.
Lines: Floating line for dries and nymphs, sink tip line for streamers.
Leaders: 12+' 4-5x for nymphs, 10' 5-7x for dries, 7' 0-2x for streamers.
Wading: Best fished by a drift boat due to the size of the river and lack of accessibility. Chest-high waders with wading belt are recommended.

Flies to Use:
Dries: Parachute Adams #16-22, BWO #18-24, Goddard's Caddis #14-18, Elk Hair Caddis #14-18, Trico #18-22, Rusty Spinner #16-20, Griffith's Gnat #18-24, Disco Midge #18-22, Cluster Midge #18-22, PMX #8-12, Parachute Hopper #6-10, Red or Black Flying Ant #16-20, Yellow Stimulator #16-18, RS-2 #18-22, Olive Sparkle Dun #16-20.
Nymphs: Brassie #18-22, Hare's Ear #16-20, Sparkle Pupa #18-20, Midge Pupa #18-22, Prince Nymph #16-18, Pheasant Tail #16-22, Lightning Bug #16-20, Serendipity #14-20, Red or Brown San Juan Worm #6-8, Pink, Orange or Olive Scud #14-20, Ray Charles #16-18, Green & Brown Bugger #2-6.
Streamers: Green, Brown, or Black Bugger #2-6, Leeches #2-8, Green, White or Natural Zonkers #2-6, JJ's Special #2-6.

Sunset on the Bighorn.
Photo by Joe Irons.

Bighorn treasure.
Photo by Brian Grossenbacher.

The character of the Bighorn is spring creek in nature with flowing weed beds, undulating currents and crystal clear waters. Because the waters of the Bighorn are taken 150' below the surface of the reservoir, the Bighorn is a true year-round fishery. Although the Bighorn enjoys prolific hatches, day in and day out anglers find the most success nymph fishing. Due to its reputation as a quality tailwater fishery, the Bighorn is crowded throughout most of the year. Start early in the morning, or plan your trip during the off-season to avoid the crowds. It is important to note that during some years excessive algae can make the Bighorn difficult to fish during September and October. Call ahead before planning your fall trip to the Bighorn.

Another nice Bighorn brown.
Photo by Joe Irons.

When to Fish:

The Bighorn is known for being a true year-round fishery. Call ahead for conditions in late fall when the algae breaks free and makes for challenging to impossible nymph and streamer fishing. If you loathe crowds, don't bother heading in that direction in the peak summer season.

Seasons & Limits:

The standard fishing regulations for the *Central* and *Eastern* fishing districts apply. Please check the *Montana Fishing Regulations and Etiquette* section.

Exceptions to Standard Regulations

Afterbay Dam to Cable 600 feet downstream and downstream from Bighorn FAS

   Open entire year.
   May use live nongame bait fish (as identified in standard district regulations).
   Combined Trout: 5 daily and in possession, only 1 over 18 inches and only 1 rainbow trout.

Cable 600 feet below Afterbay Dam to Bighorn FAS

   Open entire year.
   Combined Trout: 5 brown trout daily and in possession, only 1 over 18 inches. Catch-and-release for rainbow trout, except anglers 14 years of age and younger may take 1 rainbow trout daily and in possession, any size.
   Artificial lures only.

Nearby Fly Fishing:

Stillwater, lower Yellowstone.

Accommodations & Services:

The Bighorn Angler stakes the claim to being the oldest lodge and fly shop on the Bighorn (406-666-2233: www.bighornangler.com). Another option is Forrester's Bighorn River Resort (800-665-3799) or the Bighorn Lodge (800-235-5450: www.bighornriverlodge.com).

Rating: 9

With several thousand trout per mile, many of which are over 18", the Bighorn is a fisherman's paradise… unfortunately, the price of paradise is overcrowding.

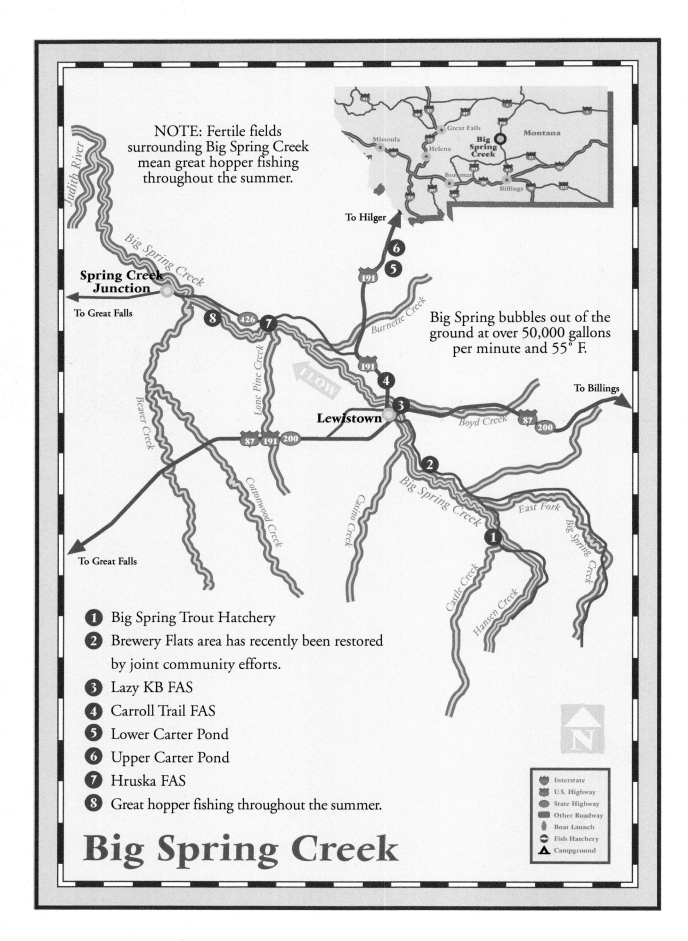

NOTE: Fertile fields surrounding Big Spring Creek mean great hopper fishing throughout the summer.

Montana

To Hilger

Big Spring bubbles out of the ground at over 50,000 gallons per minute and 55° F.

Spring Creek Junction

To Great Falls

To Billings

Lewistown

To Great Falls

FLOW

1 Big Spring Trout Hatchery

2 Brewery Flats area has recently been restored by joint community efforts.

3 Lazy KB FAS

4 Carroll Trail FAS

5 Lower Carter Pond

6 Upper Carter Pond

7 Hruska FAS

8 Great hopper fishing throughout the summer.

Big Spring Creek

Interstate
U.S. Highway
State Highway
Other Roadway
Boat Launch
Fish Hatchery
Campground

N

Big Spring Creek

Considered to be one of the few significant trout streams in Central Montana, Big Spring Creek is the third-largest freshwater spring in the world and bubbles to the earth's surface in the foothills between the Judith and Big Snowy Mountains. The cold water is quickly absorbed back into the porous strata and reemerges again at Big Spring flowing at over 50,000 gallons per minute. Once a sacred site to Native Americans, and later a valuable resource to early settlers, Big Spring Creek is still a prized water source. According to the EPA, Big Spring has been rated one of the purest springs in the U.S., and it is pumped directly into the homes of Lewistown residents without any purification. Big Spring water is also bottled and shipped across the country under a variety of labels. A portion of Big Spring is diverted and it serves as a fish hatchery in which over three million trout, including brown, rainbow and cutthroat trout, as well as kokanee salmon, are raised annually. Last but not least, Big Spring Creek is a year-round red ribbon (Class II) trout fishery that provides high-quality habitat for trout, aquatic insects, and also serves an invaluable riparian corridor to regional flora and fauna.

Big Spring Creek begins nine miles southeast of Lewistown and flows a mere 30 miles to join with the Judith River.

Big Spring brown trout heading home.
Photo by Brian Grossenbacher.

Fly fisherman on Big Spring Creek near Hruska access.
Photo by Brian Grossenbacher.

Wade fishermen will find ample access and quality fishing within a few miles of Lewistown.
Photo by Brian Grossenbacher.

It is not a large river, averaging only 35-45 feet wide and 18"-24" deep. True to its spring creek roots, Big Spring Creek is gin clear and flows over beds of vibrant green aquatic plant life. The nutrient-rich water provides an excellent habitat for aquatic insects, primarily midges, baetis and caddis with some PMD activity in June and July. The lush vegetation and surrounding hay fields allow for excellent hopper fishing from late July through September. Big Spring Creek is easy to wade, and access is prevalent throughout the upper 20 miles of the creek. The last 10 miles from Cottonwood Creek to the Judith braid and deteriorate from erosion and pollution, and is arguably not worth fishing. Regardless of where you choose to fish, make sure you watch out for rattlesnakes at all times as there are regular sightings along the entire length of this river.

Cale Van Velkinburgh warms his spirit on Big Spring Creek.
Photo by Brian Grossenbacher.

Types of Fish:
Rainbow and Brown Trout, Whitefish.

Known Hatches:
Year-round: Midges.
Late-March-June: Baetis.
April-August: Caddis.
June-August: PMDs.
June-September: Hoppers, Ants.

Equipment to Use:
Rods: 3-6 weight, 8-9 feet in length.
Lines: Floating line to match rod weight.
Leaders: 9' 3-6x for dries; 7½' 4x-5x for smaller nymphs.
Wading: Wading is easy and wet wading would be the natural choice if it weren't for the rattlesnakes. Waders are recommended.

Flies to Use:
Dries: Griffith's Gnat #20-22, Parachute Adams #16-20, Rusty Spinner #16-20, Olive Sparkle Dun #16-20, Elk Hair Caddis #14-18, Goddard Caddis #12-18, Royal Trude #12-16, Hoppers #6-12, Beetles #14-18, Ants #14-20.
Nymphs: Serendipity #16-22, Brassie #18-22, Copper John #14-18, Pheasant Tail #14-18, Hare's Ear #12-16, Prince #10-16, Lightning Bug #14-18, Sparkle Pupa #16-18, San Juan Worm #12-18.
Streamers: Woolly Bugger #4-8, Muddler Minnow #2-8, Sculpin #2-8.

When to Fish:
Spring and early summer offer good fishing with Baetis and Caddis patterns. Being a spring creek, runoff typically doesn't affect the creek although occasionally there can be discoloration from tributaries. Mid to late summer brings great hopper fishing and other terrestrial activity.

Seasons & Limits:
The standard fishing regulations for the *Central* fishing district apply. Please check the *Montana Fishing Regulations and Etiquette* section.
Exceptions to Standard Regulations
Near Lewistown
   Open entire year.
Upstream of the US Highway 191 Bridge, including East Fork Big Spring Creek downstream from the reservoir.
   Catch-and-release only for all fish species. Fish Consumption Advisory in effect.

Nearby Fly Fishing:
Upper & Lower Carter's Pond, Warm Spring Creek, Judith River, Trophy Trout Springs Ranch.

Accommodations & Services:
Just a half hour away you can stay at the Trophy Trout Springs Ranch (406-423-5542) in Hobson or try one of the Leininger Vacation cabins right outside of Lewistown (866-306-5797: www.logcabinatlewistown.com).

Rating: 7.5
Big Spring Creek is one of the few trout fishing options in Central Montana and for that reason alone it is worth fishing if you are in the area.

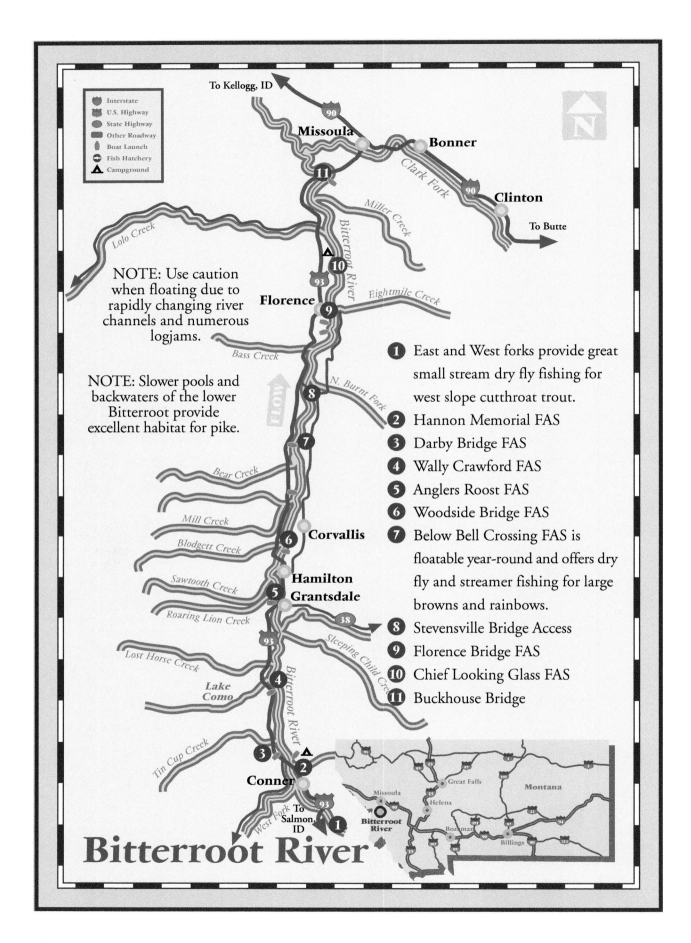

Legend:
- Interstate
- U.S. Highway
- State Highway
- Other Roadway
- Boat Launch
- Fish Hatchery
- ▲ Campground

To Kellogg, ID

Missoula

Bonner

90

Clark Fork

Clinton

To Butte

90

11

Miller Creek

Bitterroot River

10

93

Eightmile Creek

Florence

9

Lolo Creek

NOTE: Use caution when floating due to rapidly changing river channels and numerous logjams.

Bass Creek

NOTE: Slower pools and backwaters of the lower Bitterroot provide excellent habitat for pike.

LOLO

N. Burnt Fork

8

7

Bear Creek

Mill Creek

Blodgett Creek

6 **Corvallis**

Sawtooth Creek

5 **Hamilton**
Grantsdale

Roaring Lion Creek

38

Sleeping Child Creek

93

Lost Horse Creek

Lake Como

4 Bitterroot River

Tin Cup Creek

3

2 ▲

Conner

West Fork

To Salmon, ID

93

1

① East and West forks provide great small stream dry fly fishing for west slope cutthroat trout.
② Hannon Memorial FAS
③ Darby Bridge FAS
④ Wally Crawford FAS
⑤ Anglers Roost FAS
⑥ Woodside Bridge FAS
⑦ Below Bell Crossing FAS is floatable year-round and offers dry fly and streamer fishing for large browns and rainbows.
⑧ Stevensville Bridge Access
⑨ Florence Bridge FAS
⑩ Chief Looking Glass FAS
⑪ Buckhouse Bridge

Missoula
Great Falls
Helena
Montana
Bozeman
Bitterroot River
Billings

Bitterroot River

Bitterroot River

The Bitterroot comes to life at the convergence of the East and West forks of the Bitterroot respectively, just north of Conner, and continues north for 97 miles to its confluence with the Clark Fork just outside of Missoula. The Bitterroot is not large by western river standards, but its generous flow provides excellent access for the wade and float fishermen alike. The classic riffle, run and pool characteristics of the Bitterroot and abundant insect life make this river a dry fly fisherman's dream. As if that weren't enough, generous access and stunning vistas at every bend combine to make the Bitterroot a Montana favorite. Although the Bitterroot is not as fast-flowing as its regional counterparts, the Clark Fork or Rock Creek, it is notably the most dangerous of the three to float due to the rapidly changing river channels and numerous logjams. Please use caution when floating the Bitterroot, and check in with local fly shops for current river conditions.

The nutrient-rich waters of the Bitterroot offer year-round dry fly opportunities, and the Bitterroot kicks off the Montana season with the first "real" hatch of the year. While the snow is still deep in the Mountains, and many anglers are still skiing, the fishing season jumps to life on the Bitterroot in the form of a major stonefly hatch. In early April, the Skwala and Nemoura stoneflies begin to appear along with hungry trout of all sizes, eagerly trying to put on weight after the long winter's rest. This is truly an opportunity to catch 20"+ fish on a dry fly. The Bitterroot also features strong hatches of March browns, green drakes, PMDs, tricos, mahoganies, spring and fall baetis and

Enjoying the drift on one of the continent's few north flowing rivers. Photo by Brian Grossenbacher.

Types of Fish:
Rainbow, Brown, Cutthroat, Bull, and Brook Trout, Northern Pike, Whitefish.

Known Hatches:
March-April: Skwala, Nemoura and Baetis.
July: PMDs, Yellow Sallies, Green and Gray Drakes, Golden Stones and Hoppers.
August: Tricos, Spruce Moths, Hoppers and Ants.
September-October: Baetis, Mahogany Duns, Hecubas, and October Caddis.

Equipment to Use:
Rods: 4-6 weight, 8-9½ in length.
Lines: Weight forward floating lines for 95% of fishing, sink tip for streamer fishing.
Leaders: 9' 3x-4x most of the year; 10'-14' 5x-6x in late summer and fall for flat-water risers. 7½' 0-2x fluorocarbon leaders for streamers.
Wading: Chest-high waders.

Flies to Use:
Dries: Royal and Olive PMXs #10-16, Rainy's Grand Hopper, Parachute Hopper, Sparkle Dun Tricos #16-22, Parachute Adams #16-20, GT BWOs #16-20, GT Mahogany #14-16, CDC Comparadun Mahogany, Carlson's Purple Haze Parachute #14-18, Griffith's Gnats #18-22, Palomino Midge #18-22, Stimulators #8-10, Paralyzers #8-10, PMX #8-10.
Nymphs: Red Copper John #14-18, Bugmeister #6-12, Guide Chute Hare's Ear #14-18, Olive Whitlock Sculpins, Flashback Pheasant Tail #14-18, San Juan Worm, Prince Nymph #10-16, Double Bead Stones #6-8.
Streamers: JJ's Special #2-6, Olive Sculpin #2-6, dark Buggers #2-6.

When to Fish:
The Bitterroot fishes well year-round with streamers and assorted midge hatches. Once spring rolls around the Bitterroot's renowned dry fly fishing begins with Baetis, Skwalas and Nemouras. After run-off (typically early July), anglers can jump right back into dry fly fishing with everything from PMDs, Yellow Sallies, Gray and Green Drakes to hoppers and the beginning of the Tricos. Summer hatches are consistent and long. Cooler days of autumn bring with them October Caddis and Mahogany Duns, plus the return to consistent streamer fishing throughout the winter.

Seasons & Limits:
Standard fishing regulations for the *Western* fishing district apply. Please check the *Montana Fishing Regulations and Etiquette* section.
Exceptions to Standard Regulations
Ditches, Canals and Sloughs between US 93 and East Side Highway and between Hamilton and the Florence Bridge
  Regulations are the same as the adjacent river section.
Bitterroot River to the Mouth, West Fork Bitterroot River downstream from Painted Rocks Dam, and East Fork Bitterroot River downstream from Star Falls
  Extended season for northern pike and whitefish and catch-and-release for trout open December 1 to third Saturday in May with aquatic insects, maggots and/or artificial lures only.

An angler and her companion enjoy the solitude of a fall day on the Bitterroot.
Photo by Brian Grossenbacher.

October caddis, as well as explosive hopper fishing from late July through September.

The Bitterroot is paralleled by highway 93 for much of its length and is framed by the Sapphire Mountains to the east and the Bitterroot Range to the west. The cottonwood-lined banks mark the beginning of the season with faint green buds in the spring and explode in a crescendo of golden color as the season tapers off in the fall. The generous length and ready access of the Bitterroot, coupled with its close proximity to Rock Creek and the Clark Fork, distribute the pressure fairly evenly so crowding is rarely an issue, even in the height of the season.

The Bitterroot offers one of the best opportunities in the area to catch a 20"+ trout on dries during the Skwala hatch. The access is great for both wade and float fishing, although frequent log jams, blocked channels and continually-changing conditions can make it a hazardous river for floaters. The Bitterroot is a classic freestone trout stream located in a stunning valley, top that off with excellent dry fly fishing and you find yet another archetypal Rocky Mountain trout stream.

The Bitterroot is a "must fish" for dry fly aficionados.
Photo by Brian Grossenbacher.

West Fork Bitterroot River above Painted Rocks Reservoir
Catch-and release for cutthroat trout.

Painted Rocks Dam to Mouth of West Fork Bitterroot River
Combined Trout Limit: 3 rainbow or brown trout daily and in possession. Catch-and-release for cutthroat trout.

One Mile Downstream of Darby Bridge to Star Falls on the East Fork
Combined Trout: 3 rainbow or brown trout daily and in possession, 1 over 14 inches. Catch-and-release for cutthroat trout.

One Mile Downstream from Darby to Como Bridge
Catch-and-release for all trout. Artificial lures only.

Como Bridge to Tucker Crossing
Combined Trout: 3 rainbow or brown trout daily and in possession, 1 over 14 inches. Catch-and-release for cutthroat trout.

Tucker Crossing to Florence Bridge
Catch-and-release for all trout. Artificial lures only.

Florence Bridge to mouth of Bitterroot River
Combined Trout: 3 rainbow or brown trout daily and in possession, 1 over 14 inches. Catch-and-release for cutthroat trout.

Nearby Fly Fishing:

There are over 150 miles of floatable trout water within an hour of Missoula, including the Clark Fork, Blackfoot, and Rock Creek. Countless other wade-fishing opportunities exist on small streams. Great fall steelhead fishing is a stone's throw away on the Clearwater River in Idaho.

Accommodations & Services:

Many options in nearby Missoula. Below are the recommendations from the Grizzly Hackle Fly Shop.

Accommodations: DoubleTree Edgewater 406-728-3100, Holiday Inn Parkside 406-721-8550. For campers, you can find sites at Chief Looking Glass, Blodgett Park, Roaring Lion Creek, Lick Creek, Durland Park and Hannon Memorial.

Restaurants: Red Bird Café 406-549-2906, Pearl Café and Bakery 406-541-0231, Guy's Lolo Creek Steakhouse 406-273-2622, The Depot 406-728-7007, Sawaddee Thai Restaurant 406-543-9966, The Old Post 406-721-7399.

Coffee Shops: Trout River Coffee Bar (next to Grizzly Hackle) 406-721-1151.

Rating: 8

Surprisingly the Bitterroot is not ranked as one of Montana's 15 Blue Ribbon Trout Streams; however, its immediate proximity to three other Blue Ribbon fisheries, as well as its own impressive fishing, earn it a place on the Montana "must-fish" list.

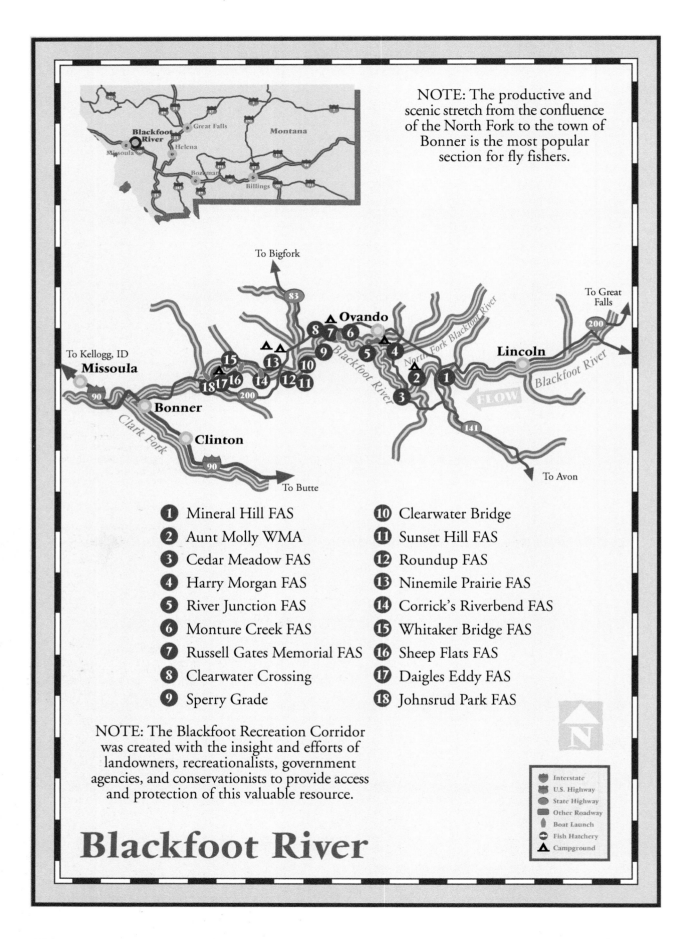

NOTE: The productive and scenic stretch from the confluence of the North Fork to the town of Bonner is the most popular section for fly fishers.

1 Mineral Hill FAS
2 Aunt Molly WMA
3 Cedar Meadow FAS
4 Harry Morgan FAS
5 River Junction FAS
6 Monture Creek FAS
7 Russell Gates Memorial FAS
8 Clearwater Crossing
9 Sperry Grade
10 Clearwater Bridge
11 Sunset Hill FAS
12 Roundup FAS
13 Ninemile Prairie FAS
14 Corrick's Riverbend FAS
15 Whitaker Bridge FAS
16 Sheep Flats FAS
17 Daigles Eddy FAS
18 Johnsrud Park FAS

NOTE: The Blackfoot Recreation Corridor was created with the insight and efforts of landowners, recreationalists, government agencies, and conservationists to provide access and protection of this valuable resource.

Interstate
U.S. Highway
State Highway
Other Roadway
Boat Launch
Fish Hatchery
Campground

Blackfoot River

Blackfoot River

A beautiful river by anyone's standards, the Blackfoot has more than just good looks. It has sheer pull-yourself-up-by-your-bootstrap guts, and a remarkable comeback story. If you are looking for the epitome of Western trout streams you'll find it right here, nestled in the Blackfoot River Valley between the Swan and Garnet mountain ranges just east of the Continental Divide, and the thriving university town of Missoula on Highway 200.

With more than 132 miles of undammed, trout-laden water between its source in the Bob Marshall Wilderness and its confluence with the Clark Fork River at Bonner, it is hard to believe that this river was nearly void of life thirty years ago. In fact, the movie *A River Runs Through It,* was based upon Norman MacLean's novel set on the Blackfoot River. However, due to years of abuse from extractive industries, the Blackfoot was unable to play the starring role in its own movie. Instead, the producers chose to shoot the majority of the movie on the scenic Gallatin River near Bozeman.

Thanks to the grassroots conservation efforts of the nationally-recognized group The Blackfoot Challenge, partnering with the Blackfoot Chapter of Trout Unlimited, the river has staged an almost inconceivable comeback. The Blackfoot Challenge united an eclectic group of concerned citizens, including local ranchers, outfitters, miners, conservation groups and government agencies, all with the common goal of

Types of Fish:
Brown, Rainbow, Cutthroat, Brook, and Bull Trout, Northern Pike, Whitefish.

Known Hatches:
Year-round: Midges. *Mid March-Late April:* Skwalas. *Mid June-Mid July:* Salmonflies; Golden Stones. *September-October:* October Caddis.

Equipment to Use:
Rods: 5-6 weight, 8½-9 ½ feet in length.
Lines: Weight forward floating lines for dries & nymphs, heavy sink tips for streamers. *Leaders:* 9' 3x for nymphs, 9' 4x-5x for dries, 7½' 0-2x fluorocarbon for streamers. *Wading:* Chest-high waders and wading belt with felt-soled boots recommended for all but late summer when some wet wading may be possible. A tricky river to wade due to deep pools and swift currents.

Flies to Use:
Dries: Sofa Pillows #2-4, Rogue Stones #2-6, Jacklin's Stone #2-10, Orange Stimulators #6-10, Paralyzers #8-10, Chernobyl Ant & Hopper #6-10, PMX #8-12, Triple Decker #6-10. *Nymphs*: Kaufman Stone #2-6, Bitch Creek #2-6, Double Bead Stonefly #2-10, San Juan Worm #6-10. *Streamers*: Olive Sculpin #4-6, JJ Special #4-6, Double Bunnies #4-6.

When to Fish:
The salmonfly hatch mid June to mid July is always memorable. Streamers are great during April and again in October. However, make sure not to fish extra-heavy rods and large streamers (4 or bigger) as these will get you in trouble for attempting to catch bull trout. During the summer the river can get crowded.

The spectacular scenery and resurgent trout population are putting the Blackfoot back on the map.

Cooperative efforts are helping to restore the Blackfoot to its former glory.
Photo by Brian Grossenbacher.

restoring the Blackfoot. For anyone searching for an inspiring story of community cooperation, look no further. For those of you looking for a trout grand slam —cutthroat, rainbows, bulls, and browns—you too can end your search.

The Blackfoot River has frequent and easy access along Highway 200. The fishing season kicks off with the Skwala hatch in April and culminates with quality streamer fishing in November. The Blackfoot offers especially good fishing after runoff in June and July, with an epic salmonfly hatch and classic hopper fishing in late summer. Other hatches include golden stones, green drakes, caddis and both fall and spring baetis. Most anglers concentrate on the 60 miles of blue ribbon fishing from the junction of the North Fork to the town of Bonner. The Blackfoot courses through canyons of sheer rock cliffs, enchanting meadows, and towering ponderosa forests. With thirty-plus miles of the Blackfoot River Recreation Corridor, numerous camping options, and the charming town of Ovando on its northern bank, the Blackfoot offers everything you need. Cutthroat average anywhere from 10"-16", rainbows from 12"-19" and browns frequently push the 20" mark. The Blackfoot also supports a recovering population of the threatened bull trout. Fishing for bull trout is prohibited, and if caught inadvertently, they should be immediately released.

A healthy brown trout made possible by the efforts of The Blackfoot Challenge. Photo by Brian Grossenbacher.

Seasons & Limits:

The standard fishing regulations for the *Western* fishing district apply. Please check the *Montana Fishing Regulations and Etiquette* section.

Exceptions to Standard Regulations

Year-round fishing with the following exceptions:

Entire River and Tributaries except Clearwater River

Combined Trout: 3 daily and in possession, no rainbow trout over 12 inches, any size brown trout. (See Clearwater River Drainage for exception.) Catch-and-release for cutthroat trout. Artificial lures only within 100-yard radius of the mouths of Belmont Creek, Gold Creek, Monture Creek and North Fork Blackfoot River.

Mainstem Only

Extended season for northern pike and whitefish and catch-and-release for trout open December 1 to third Saturday in May with artificial lures and/or maggots only. Tributaries are closed to fishing.

Landers Fork Mouth to Stimson Lumber Dam (Milltown Reservoir)

Catch-and-release for brook trout. (This regulation is a result of bull trout being misidentified and harvested as brook trout. Brook trout are very rare in this section of river whereas bull trout are common.)

Stimson Lumber Dam Downstream to Milltown Reservoir (Clark Fork River)

Northern pike: no limit. Extended season for northern pike from December 1 to third Saturday in May, with artificial lures only.

Nearby Fly Fishing:

Clark Fork, Bitterroot, Rock Creek, Missouri, Brown Lake, N. Fork of Blackfoot, Clearwater River.

Accommodations & Services:

The Blackfoot has many camping opportunities along the river, including Gold Creek, the Blackfoot Recreation Corridor, Russell Gates, and River Junction. The Blackfoot Inn (406-793-5555: www.blackfoot-inn.com) in Ovando is homey and hospitable. Peggy and Howie Fly are charming hosts and you'll feel as if you've stepped back in time 50 years. If you are looking for the complete fly fishing experience, check in with Paul Roos' North Fork Angler (800-858-3497: www.paulroosoutfitters.com) which offers a gourmet chef, and high-end wall tents on the banks of the North Fork. As for dinner, you can't beat the experience at Trixie's (406-793-5611) in Ovando.

Rating: 8

The Blackfoot is a timeless, freestone river that ranks a hearty 9 if you are solely focused on scenery, experience and great floating. The fishing can be fantastic in early and late season, but can be marginal during summer due to heat and crowds from Missoula, especially in the lower stretches of the river. Fishing alone is a 7, however the proximity to multiple other blue ribbon trout streams helps to round the Blackfoot out at a solid 8.

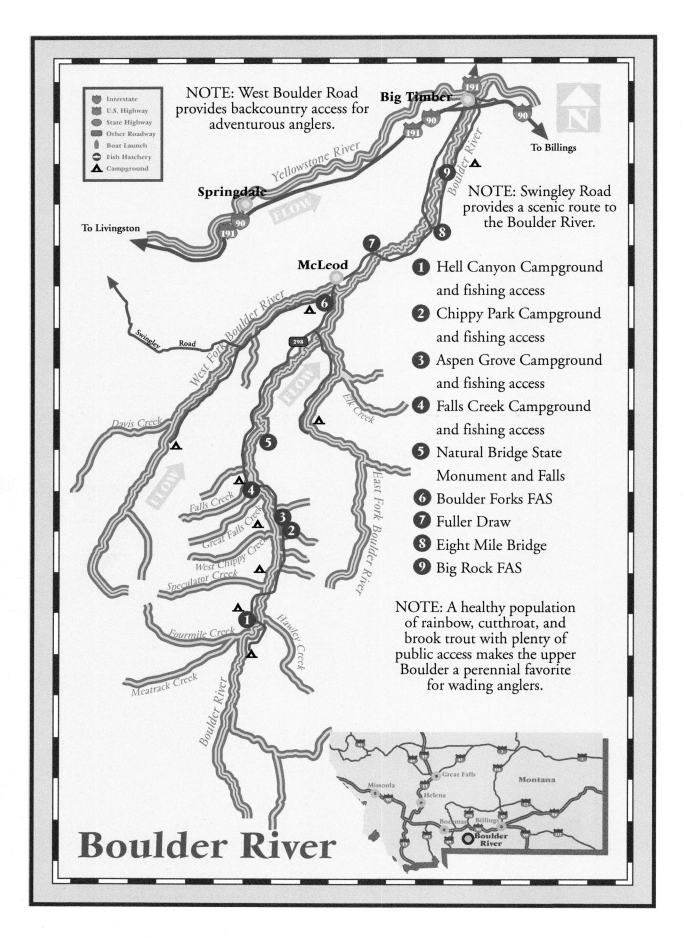

NOTE: West Boulder Road provides backcountry access for adventurous anglers.

NOTE: Swingley Road provides a scenic route to the Boulder River.

1 Hell Canyon Campground and fishing access

2 Chippy Park Campground and fishing access

3 Aspen Grove Campground and fishing access

4 Falls Creek Campground and fishing access

5 Natural Bridge State Monument and Falls

6 Boulder Forks FAS

7 Fuller Draw

8 Eight Mile Bridge

9 Big Rock FAS

NOTE: A healthy population of rainbow, cutthroat, and brook trout with plenty of public access makes the upper Boulder a perennial favorite for wading anglers.

Interstate
U.S. Highway
State Highway
Other Roadway
Boat Launch
Fish Hatchery
Campground

Big Timber
To Billings
To Livingston
Springdale
McLeod
Yellowstone River
Boulder River
West Fork Boulder River
Swingley Road
Davis Creek
Falls Creek
Great Falls Creek
West Chippy Creek
Speculator Creek
Fourmile Creek
Meatrack Creek
Boulder River
Hawley Creek
Elk Creek
East Fork Boulder River

Boulder River

Montana
Great Falls
Missoula
Helena
Bozeman
Billings
Boulder River

Boulder River

Next to the definition of "Trout Stream" in the dictionary, there is a picture of the Boulder River. Gin clear water tumbles over perfectly rounded rocks, surrounded by stands of lodgepole pine and aspen groves, gracefully dividing the Absaroka and Beartooth Mountains. When fishing the Boulder River, anglers can truly feel as if they have stepped back in time—no subdivisions, no traffic, just healthy trout, dirt roads, remarkable vistas, and solitude.

The Boulder can be accessed easily from either Big Timber or Livingston. We strongly recommend the path less traveled via the drive on Swingley Road out of Livingston. This well-maintained gravel road traverses mountain meadows, stunning vistas, century plus old ranches, and delivers you to the banks of the lush, and tumbling West Boulder River. If you are looking for a hike, drive up the Forest Service access road you'll find just shortly after crossing the West Boulder. After 7 miles you'll reach the trail head where you can embark on a fairly easy three-mile hike up to a rarely-fished stretch of the West Boulder. If you are an avid backcountry fly fisher or simply a lover of the out-of-doors, you'll find this hike well worth your time.

Traveling on from the West Boulder on Swingley road you'll eventually come to a T, where McLeod road from Big Timber intersects. Although the Boulder River is not known for its easy

Types of Fish:
Rainbow, Brown, Cutthroat, and Brook Trout, Whitefish.

Known Hatches:
January-March: Midges (Diptera).
Late February-Early March: Black Stoneflies.
Late-April: Blue-Winged Olives (Baetis), March Browns, Caddis.
June: Golden Stones, Yellow Sallies.
Mid-July-August: Caddis, Pale Morning Duns, Brown Drakes, Hoppers, Ants.

Equipment to Use:
Rods: 4-6 weight, 8-9 feet in length.
Lines: Floating line to match rod weight.
Leaders: 9' 5x for dries, 7½' 3x for big nymphs, 4-5x for smaller nymphs, 7½' 0-2x fluorocarbon for streamers.
Wading: Chest-high waders with felt-soled boots for most of season. Wading can be tricky due to swift current and numerous boulders. Wet-wading is possible late July-August.

Flies to Use:
Dries: Griffith's Gnat #20-22, Red Quill #12-16, Parachute Adams #16-20, Rusty Spinner #16-22, Olive Sparkle Dun #16-20, Elk Hair Caddis #14-16, Goddard Caddis #12-16, Stimulator #8-10, Yellow Sally #14-16, Royal Trude #12-16, Hoppers #6-12, Beetles #14-18, Ants #10-20.
(Continued)

Jenny Grossenbacher nymphs the deep pockets of the Boulder.
Photo by Brian Grossenbacher.

Fish on! Hitting the deep pockets pays off.
Photo by Brian Grossenbacher.

public access, either direction will lead you to enough options to entertain an angler for a day. Turn left (North) and you'll find a couple of access points, including Boulder Forks and Big Rock, both maintained fishing access sites, as well as access via Fuller Draw, and Eight Mile bridge, respectively. Even before you can wade out of sight of the bridges you'll be into some great pocket fishing with your choice of healthy rainbows. As long as you stay below the high-water mark, you can wade as far as you are game.

Turning right (South) at the main Boulder road you'll not only find several access and camping sites, you'll also find the Natural Bridge State Monument, a geologic wonder where the river briefly flows entirely underground. The fish on the Boulder are not picky and will rise enthusiastically to attractor patterns, hoppers, beetles and ants during the summer months, and general nymphs such as bead head princes, copper Johns, and girdle bugs year-round.

Brian Grossenbacher at the Boulder River on a summer day.
Photo by Jenny Grossenbacher.

Flies to Use: (Continued)

Nymphs: Serendipity #16-22, Brassie #18-22, Copper John #14-18, Pheasant Tail #14-18, Hare's Ear #12-16, Prince #10-16, Lightning Bug #14-18, Sparkle Pupa #16-18, Kaufmann's Golden Stones #8-12, Brown Rubber Legs #8-12.
Streamers: Woolly Bugger #4-8, Muddler Minnow #2-8, Sculpin #2-8.

When to Fish:

Spring and early summer offer several hatches, including baetis and caddis. Runoff typically arrives in late May to early June, and sometimes lasts into early July. Mid to late summer brings great hopper fishing and other terrestrial activity. Fall can be even better with the browns from the Yellowstone moving up into the lower reaches of the Boulder.

Seasons & Limits:

The standard fishing regulations for the *Central* fishing district apply. Please check the *Montana Fishing Regulations and Etiquette* section.
Exceptions to Standard Regulations
Entire River and Tributaries:
   Open entire year.
   Combined Trout: 2 daily and in possession, only 1 over 13 inches.
Natural Bridge to Two-Mile Bridge (First Crossing, 5 Road Miles Upstream from Natural Bridge)
   Catch-and-release for rainbow trout, except anglers 14 years of age and younger may take 1 rainbow trout daily and in possession, any size. Artificial lures only.

Nearby Fly Fishing:

West Boulder, Yellowstone River, high alpine lakes and creeks in Beartooth Wilderness.

Accommodations & Services:

Try the Grand Hotel in Big Timber (406-932-4459: www.thegrand-hotel.com) for both lodging and a fantastic dinner. There are cabins and camping in McLeod at the Mcleod Resort (www.mcleodmt.com). There are several campgrounds along the river, including Boulder Forks, Falls Creek, Big Beaver, Aspen, Hell's Canyon, Lower Fourmile and the campground at the West Boulder River National Forest Access.

Rating: 8

For beauty and solitude alone the Boulder is a river not to be missed. It is a magical, pristine, high-mountain stream with a beautiful backdrop. Tons of pocket water, deep pools, and short runs make for great holding water for 10-18+" trout and serve as a nymph fisherman's delight. Limited access in the lower stretches and difficult wading and floating are some of the challenges.

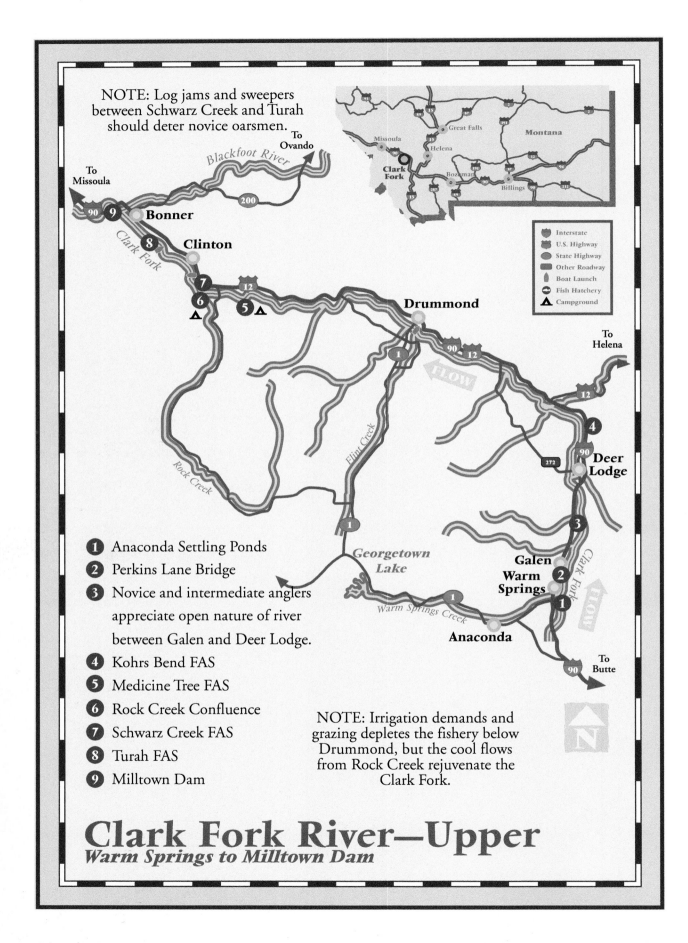

NOTE: Log jams and sweepers between Schwarz Creek and Turah should deter novice oarsmen.

Montana

Interstate
U.S. Highway
State Highway
Other Roadway
Boat Launch
Fish Hatchery
Campground

1 Anaconda Settling Ponds
2 Perkins Lane Bridge
3 Novice and intermediate anglers appreciate open nature of river between Galen and Deer Lodge.
4 Kohrs Bend FAS
5 Medicine Tree FAS
6 Rock Creek Confluence
7 Schwarz Creek FAS
8 Turah FAS
9 Milltown Dam

NOTE: Irrigation demands and grazing depletes the fishery below Drummond, but the cool flows from Rock Creek rejuvenate the Clark Fork.

Clark Fork River—Upper
Warm Springs to Milltown Dam

Clark Fork River
Warm Springs to Milltown Dam

The Clark Fork River is a living paradox. In spite of its origin at the base of the largest superfund site in the United States, it still maintains a rich population of aquatic life throughout much of its length. The upper section generally resembles a spring creek with clear water, easy wading, nutrient-rich water, and a healthy population of wily brown trout. As the Clark Fork heads west it continues to absorb tributaries such as the Little Blackfoot, Flint Creek, Rock Creek and shortly before the Milltown Dam the Blackfoot River. Not only do these tributaries breathe new life into the Clark Fork, but each radically enhances its flow and character eventually forming the largest river in the state.

The upper section to Galen twists and turns and offers up to 1,500 trout per mile—impressive numbers due to the small size of the stream and the aforementioned environmental abuse. A short rod may help you to overcome the constant hazard of heavy overhanging brush that challenges even the most accurate casters. Access is excellent throughout the Warm Springs Wildlife Management Area, although float fishing is not permitted until the Perkins Lane Bridge at mile 3.5.

The river opens and gains volume downstream from Galen, however, due to lower flows and higher water temperatures during summertime irrigation, the fish counts drop slightly. Even still, the wading is easy in this section, access is good at county road bridge crossings and the average size of the trout increases

Types of Fish:
Rainbow, Brown, Brook, and Westslope Cutthroat, Whitefish, Northern Pike.

Known Hatches:
Year round: Midges.
Late March-June: Baetis, Skwala Stone, Caddis, Cranefly, Green & Brown Drakes.
June-July: Caddis, Salmonfly, PMD, Hoppers, Yellow Sally.
July-August: Caddis, PMD, Green & Brown Drakes, Yellow Sally, Hoppers, Ants, Beetles.
August-September: Trico, Caddis.
September-October: Mahogany Dun, Streamers.

Equipment to Use:
Rods: 5-7 weight, 8-9 feet in length.
Lines: Weight forward floating for dry fly and nymph fishing, sinking tips for streamers.
Leaders: 7½' 2-4x for nymphing, 9' 4-6x for dry fly, 7½' 1x-2x for streamers.
Wading: Relatively easy; chest-high waders.

Flies to Use:
Dries: Parachute Adams #12-20, Blue Winged Olives #18-20, Griffith's Gnat #18-22, Parachute Adams #16-20, Parachute Hopper #4-10, PMD Sparkle Dun #14-18, Compardun #14-18, Lt. Cahill #14-18, Ant #14-16, Stimulator #8-14.
Nymphs: Hare's Ear #12-18, Prince Nymph #10-16, Brooks Stone #4-10, Kaufman's Stone #4-10, Midge Pupa #18-22, Pheasant Tail Nymph #16-20, Beadhead Copper John #16, Lightning Bug #16-18.
Streamers: Woolly Bugger #2-8, JJ Special #2-6, Muddler Minnow #2-6.

The upper stretches of the Clark Fork resemble a spring creek.
Photo by Brian Grossenbacher.

A healthy population of wild brown trout exist in the upper Clark Fork in spite of generations of environmental abuses. Photo by Brian Grossenbacher.

slightly to around 14 inches with much larger fish present. Beginner and intermediate anglers may appreciate the open nature of this section, and can concentrate more on fishing and spend less time in the brush. This upper section downstream to Deer Lodge is difficult to float in anything larger than a personal watercraft or maneuverable canoe with experienced paddlers.

Downstream from Deer Lodge the Clark Fork continues to suffer from irrigation related temperature issues and fish numbers drop significantly. The exceptions occur downstream from the Little Blackfoot and Flint Creek where much needed flows of cooler, oxygenated water revitalize the Clark Fork and its trout. From Drummond to Clinton the river loses virtually all of its appeal as a trout fishery with the exception of early and late season streamer fishing, when migratory trout move into this area to spawn.

At Clinton, the cooler flows of Rock Creek substantially improve the fishing conditions of the Clark Fork, and it once again shines as a viable trout fishery with healthy populations of rainbow, brown and westslope cutthroat trout. The river is much larger in this section giving the advantage to float fishermen, but there are still plenty of wadeable riffles for the enthusiastic wading angler. Maintained ramps at Clinton (Schwartz Creek) and Turah provide an excellent float, although braided channels, sweepers and log jams should deter inexperienced oarsmen.

Despite the four Superfund sites along its length, the aquatic insect life on the Clark Fork is as prolific as any river in the state. Multiple caddis hatches occur throughout the season, and the skwalas and salmonflies provide excellent action in the spring and early summer. Other major hatches include March browns, PMDs, hoppers, tricos, mahoganies and baetis.

Evening on the Clark Fork.
Photo by Brian Grossenbacher.

When to Fish:
With the length and diversity of fishing on the Clark Fork practically any time of year except spring run-off (typically late April to mid June) can produce good fishing. Early spring presents solid fishing and the summer months offer great opportunities for numerous dry fly hatches. Fall is the best time for streamer fishermen.

Seasons & Limits:
The standard fishing regulations for the *Western* fishing district apply. Please check the *Montana Fishing Regulations and Etiquette* section.
Exceptions to Standard Regulations
Upstream from Perkins Lane Bridge (Near Warm Springs)
    Artificial lures only. Catch-and-release only. Open entire year. Closed to fishing from boats.
Perkins Lane Bridge (Near Warm Springs) to mouth of Flathead River
    Northern pike: no limit.
    Extended season for northern pike and whitefish and catch-and-release for trout open December 1 to third Saturday in May with artificial lures and/or maggots only. Catch-and-release for trout. Combined Trout: 3 daily and in possession, none over 15 inches. Artificial lures only within a 100-yard radius of the mouths of Rattlesnake Creek, Petty Creek, Fish Creek, Cedar Creek, Dry Creek, Trout Creek and St. Regis River.
Mouth of Flathead River to mouth of Thompson River
    Catch-and-release for cutthroat trout.
    Whitefish: open entire year with maggots or lures.
    Northern pike: open entire year with bait or lures.
Mouth of Thompson River to Idaho Border
    Open entire year. Western District Standard Limits apply to entire reach.

Nearby Fly Fishing:
Warm Springs Ponds, Big Hole, Beaverhead, Georgetown Lake, Bitterroot.

Accommodations & Services:
If starting at the headwaters, Anaconda offers the family-friendly Fairmont Hot Springs (800-663-4979: www.fairmonthotsprings.com). Missoula offers countless options as well (see the Bitterroot sidebar).

Rating: 7.5
It's hard to rate a river full of toxic mining tailings too highly…yet, oddly enough, there are great browns in this river and numerous opportunities to have excellent and varied fishing almost year-round. The fate of the Clark Fork is sure to change with the extensive reclamation in progress, so check in with local fly shops before visiting.

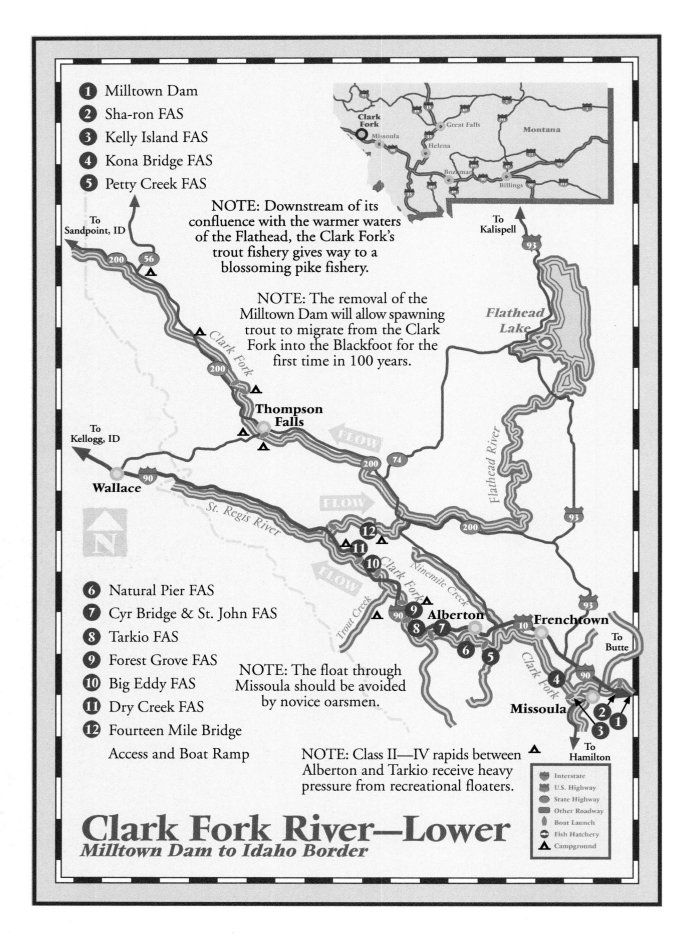

1 Milltown Dam
2 Sha-ron FAS
3 Kelly Island FAS
4 Kona Bridge FAS
5 Petty Creek FAS

NOTE: Downstream of its confluence with the warmer waters of the Flathead, the Clark Fork's trout fishery gives way to a blossoming pike fishery.

NOTE: The removal of the Milltown Dam will allow spawning trout to migrate from the Clark Fork into the Blackfoot for the first time in 100 years.

To Sandpoint, ID

To Kellogg, ID

To Kalispell

Flathead Lake

Clark Fork

Thompson Falls

Wallace

Flathead River

FLOW

FLOW

FLOW

St. Regis River

Ninemile Creek

6 Natural Pier FAS
7 Cyr Bridge & St. John FAS
8 Tarkio FAS
9 Forest Grove FAS
10 Big Eddy FAS
11 Dry Creek FAS
12 Fourteen Mile Bridge Access and Boat Ramp

Trout Creek

Clark Fork

Alberton

Frenchtown

To Butte

Clark Fork

Missoula

NOTE: The float through Missoula should be avoided by novice oarsmen.

NOTE: Class II—IV rapids between Alberton and Tarkio receive heavy pressure from recreational floaters.

To Hamilton

Interstate
U.S. Highway
State Highway
Other Roadway
Boat Launch
Fish Hatchery
Campground

Clark Fork River—Lower
Milltown Dam to Idaho Border

Clark Fork River
Milltown Dam to Idaho Border

Despite the environmental atrocities upstream, the Clark Fork from Missoula to the Idaho border is a recreationalist's dream. Pleasure floaters, whitewater enthusiasts and fishermen alike find sanctity in the clear water, scenic landscape and ready access. Due to the large volume of water compared to its relatively low fish count, most anglers prefer to float this section of the Clark Fork. Although the numbers are low, the fish tend to pod up in the Clark Fork, and once you begin to recognize their holding water, you will find ample numbers. Do not be afraid to keep the boat moving until you spot likely water or feeding fish. Pods are often separated by several hundred yards of dead water. Look for any seams, current breaks and incoming tributaries. Clark Fork trout are not shy to take dry flies, and pods can often be spotted by their dimpling surface takes. There are some truly large trout on the Clark Fork, and very large fish in the 25+ inch range are caught each season.

Wading anglers may want to concentrate on the riprap banks near Clinton and Turah, or the easily accessible and surprisingly productive water through Missoula. Downstream wading opportunities include Kelly Island, Kona Bridge, Petty Creek and Cyr.

The dry fly season starts early on the Clark Fork with a productive skwala hatch in early April, along with baetis, and a prolific caddis hatch. Like the Yellowstone, the Clark Fork is a

Types of Fish:
Rainbow, Brown, Brook, and Westslope Cutthroat, Northern Pike, Smallmouth Bass, Whitefish.

Known Hatches:
Year round: Midges.
Late March-June: Baetis, Skwala Stone, Caddis, Cranefly, Green & Brown Drakes.
June-July: Caddis, Salmonfly, PMD, Hoppers, Yellow Sally.
July-August: Caddis, PMD, Green & Brown Drakes, Yellow Sally, Hoppers, Ants, Beetles.
August-September: Trico, Caddis.
September-October: Mahogany Dun, Streamers.

Equipment to Use:
Rods: 5-8 weight, 8-9 feet in length.
Lines: Weight forward floating for dry fly and nymph fishing, high-density sinking tips for streamers.
Leaders: 7½' 2-4x for nymphing, 9' 4-6x for dry fly, 7' 0x-2x for streamers (steel tippet for pike).
Wading: Relatively easy; chest-high waders.

Flies to Use:
Dries: Parachute Adams #12-20, Blue Winged Olives #18-20, Griffith's Gnat #18-22, Parachute Adams #16-20, Parachute Hopper #4-10, PMD Sparkle Dun #14-18, Compardun #14-18, Lt. Cahill #14-18, Ant #14-16, Stimulator #8-14.
Nymphs: Hare's Ear #12-18, Prince Nymph #10-16, Brooks Stone #4-10, Kaufman's Stone #4-10, Midge Pupa #18-22, Pheasant Tail Nymph #16-20, Beadhead Copper John #16, Lightning Bug #16-18.
Streamers: Woolly Bugger #2-8, JJ Special #2-6, Muddler Minnow #2-6.

Evening on the Clark Fork near Cyr.
Photo by Brian Grossenbacher.

Look for the pods of fish taking advantage of the healthy insect population of the Clark Fork. Photo by Brian Grossenbacher.

first class hopper fishery from late July through mid-September. The season ends with mahogany duns, a healthy fall baetis hatch and excellent streamer fishing. It should be noted that the Clark Fork has the best population and longest lasting golden stone hatch in the Missoula area. They're huge (some a #6), and they are a reliable food source all the way through September.

Rainbow trout are the predominate species along with brown and westslope cutthroat trout, but there are also numerous pike in the backwaters and slower sections that will readily take large rabbit streamers stripped.

Access is available immediately below the Milltown dam providing a short, non-technical float to Sha-ron. The float through Missoula is not an easy one to negotiate, due to a large diversion dam, multiple log jams, and possible portages. If you are not familiar with this section, it should be avoided. The increased flows from the Blackfoot and the Bitterroot Rivers substantially increase the size of the Clark Fork.

The Clark Fork runs at a steady pace until it hits the town of Alberton and the real white water begins. From Alberton to the Tarkio access white water ranges from Class II to IV, and receives heavy pressure from recreational floaters. This section should only be attempted by competent whitewater oarsmen. The deep pools and pocket water in this section provide excellent holding water and the fish counts climb accordingly. Although the fish spread out again below Tarkio, quality fishing continues until the confluence of the Flathead. Generally the water below the Flathead confluence is too warm to be a viable trout fishery. From this point to the Idaho border, the Clark Fork widens and slows and runs through a chain of lakes providing excellent pike habitat.

Anglers, recreationalists and conservationists are truly excited by removal of the Milltown Dam, but also maintain an air of caution. Questions abound as millions of cubic yards of contaminated sediment behind the Milltown Dam are set to be removed. If all goes as planned, the Clark Fork trout will once again migrate and spawn upstream into the Blackfoot, Upper Clark Fork and Rock Creek. Fish populations should soar, and the health of the Clark Fork and upstream drainages will flourish. Some areas of the river will be closed during the dam's removal.

Although both the Montana Fish Wildlife and Parks and Envirocon, the Missoula based environmental clean-up company contracted to perform the work, have promised to take all possible precautions to limit or eliminate toxic material being flushed into the lower Clark Fork, many "what if," questions still linger. Only time will tell how well the Clark Fork will fare in the short term. In the meantime we will all have to hope for the best and focus on the long-term benefits of a healthy Clark Fork.

When to Fish:
The length and diversity of the Clark Fork can produce good fishing practically any time of year, except spring run-off (typically late April to mid June). Early spring presents solid fishing and the summer months offer great opportunities for numerous dry fly hatches and great hopper fishing. Fall is the best time for streamer fishermen.

Seasons & Limits:
The standard fishing regulations for the *Western* fishing district apply. Please check the *Montana Fishing Regulations and Etiquette* section.

Exceptions to Standard Regulations

Upstream from Perkins Lane Bridge (Near Warm Springs)
   Artificial lures only. Catch-and-release only. Open entire year. Closed to fishing from boats.

Perkins Lane Bridge (Near Warm Springs) to mouth of Flathead River
   Northern pike: no limit.
   Extended season for northern pike and whitefish and catch-and-release for trout open December 1 to third Saturday in May with artificial lures and/or maggots only. Catch-and-release for cutthroat trout. Combined Trout: 3 daily and in possession, none over 15 inches. Artificial lures only within a 100-yard radius of the mouths of Rattlesnake Creek, Petty Creek, Fish Creek, Cedar Creek, Dry Creek, Trout Creek and St. Regis River.

Mouth of Flathead River to mouth of Thompson River
   Catch-and-release for cutthroat trout.
   Whitefish: open entire year with maggots or lures.
   Northern pike: open entire year with bait or lures.

Mouth of Thompson River to Idaho Border
   Open entire year. Western District Standard Limits apply to entire reach.

Nearby Fly Fishing:
Bitterroot, Blackfoot, Rock Creek, Kootenai, Yaak, Swan.

Accommodations & Services:
There are numerous options in Missoula (see Bitterroot and Blackfoot sidebars) for a start. Also, try the Clark Fork Lodge in Clinton (800-580-9703: www.clarkforkriverlodge.com).

Rating: 7.5
The fate of the Clark Fork is sure to change with the heralded removal of the Milltown dam. Check in with local fly shops before visiting.

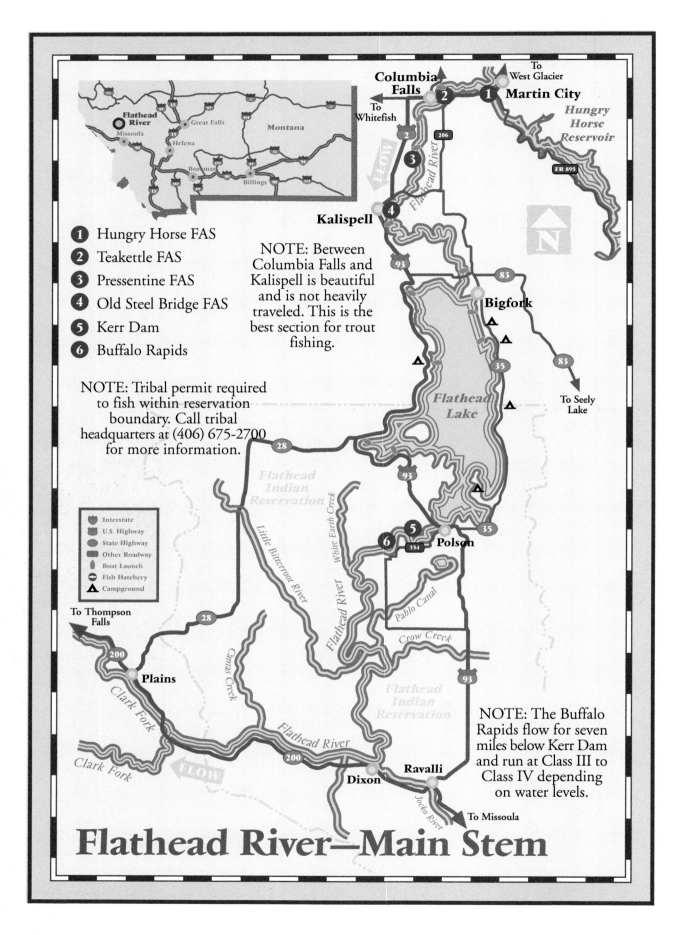

To
West Glacier

Columbia Falls

Martin City

Hungry Horse Reservoir

To Whitefish

Flathead River

Kalispell

1 Hungry Horse FAS

2 Teakettle FAS

3 Pressentine FAS

4 Old Steel Bridge FAS

5 Kerr Dam

6 Buffalo Rapids

NOTE: Between Columbia Falls and Kalispell is beautiful and is not heavily traveled. This is the best section for trout fishing.

Bigfork

Flathead Lake

To Seely Lake

NOTE: Tribal permit required to fish within reservation boundary. Call tribal headquarters at (406) 675-2700 for more information.

Flathead Indian Reservation

White Earth Creek

Little Bitterroot River

Interstate
U.S. Highway
State Highway
Other Roadway
Boat Launch
Fish Hatchery
Campground

6 **5** **Polson**

Pablo Canal

Crow Creek

To Thompson Falls

Camas Creek

Plains

Clark Fork

Flathead River

Clark Fork

Dixon **Ravalli**

Flathead Indian Reservation

NOTE: The Buffalo Rapids flow for seven miles below Kerr Dam and run at Class III to Class IV depending on water levels.

Jocko River

To Missoula

Flathead River—Main Stem

Flathead River
Main Stem

The main stem of the Flathead begins at Blankenship Bridge where the North Fork and Middle Fork of the Flathead come together. The South Fork of the Flathead joins shortly downstream to complete the triad. The massive river drains most of Glacier National Park, the Bob Marshall Wilderness, and the Flathead National Forest. The Flathead River flows for nearly 160 miles and eventually dumps into the Clark Fork River near Paradise. The river is distinctly divided into two sections separated by Flathead Lake—the largest natural lake west of the Mississippi.

The upper Flathead above the lake certainly offers the best trout fishing with a moderate population of rainbow, and westslope cutthroat trout as well as the occasional bull and lake trout. The water runs cold most of the year and sometimes is tinted with blue/green glacial sediment. Although the river does not have prolific hatches, the fish will rise enthusiastically to dry flies. The best hatches are caddis which occur throughout the summer. Look for stoneflies early season, and hoppers later in the summer, but don't fret too much about matching the hatch on the Flathead. Most importantly any attractor pattern with a

Types of Fish:
Rainbow, Westslope Cutthroat, Bull, Brown and Lake Trout, Northern Pike, Smallmouth Bass, Whitefish.

Known Hatches:
Year-round: Midges.
Mid March-Early June: Baetis.
May-June: Salmonflies.
May-September: Caddis.
June-July: Golden Stones; Green, Grey & Brown Drakes.
June-September: PMDs.
Late June-September: Hoppers, Ants.
August-September: Tricos; Spruce Moths; Craneflies.
Mid September-October: Baetis.

Equipment to Use:
Rods: 5-7 weight, 8½-9 in length.
Lines: Weight forward floating for dry fly and nymph fishing, high-density sinking tips, and/or full sinking lines for streamers.
Leaders: 9' 4x-6x for dry flies, 7½' 3-5 x for nymphing, 7½' 0-2x for streamers and steel tippet for pike.
Wading: The Main Stem of the Flathead is a massive river, and truly demands a floating craft—even if just for transportation to get to wadeable riffles. Anything from a motor boat to a personal water craft will give anglers the upper hand at covering this large body of water.

The Flathead River near Columbia Falls.
Photo by Brian Grossenbacher.

Fishing an evening caddis hatch on the Flathead.
Photo by Brian Grossenbacher.

drag free drift will get attention.

Immediately below the lake at Kerr Dam, the river rushes quickly through the Buffalo Rapids for the first 7 miles. This water is rated between Class III and Class IV. Below the rapids the river more or less resembles a moving lake, and pike fishing is the main attraction. Large rabbit stripped streamers cast into the grassy banks and retrieved quickly can yield explosive action. The best times for pike fishing occur in the early summer and fall when the pike move into the shallows.

The sheer volume of the Flathead River throughout its length makes it a difficult river for wading anglers. Floating is definitely the way to fish this river. The good news is that with few exceptions the Flathead moves quickly, but at a manageable pace and is suitable for most reliable watercraft—including personal pontoon boats when conditions allow.

A visit by a PMD aids in matching the hatch.
Photo by Brian Grossenbacher.

Flies to Use:

Dries: Royal Wulff #12-16, Parachute Pheasant Tail #14-16, Blue Winged Olives #18-20, Griffith's Gnat #18-22, Parachute Adams #16-20, Parachute Hopper #10, PMD Sparkle Dun #16, EC Caddis #14-18, Ant #14-16.
Nymphs: Tunghead Prince Nymph #14, Brown Tunghead Stonefly Nymph #14, Tunghead Midge Pupa #18-22, Lime Green Midge #20-22, Brassie #18-24 Pheasant Tail Nymph #16-20, Beadhead Copper John #14-16, Lightning Bug #16-18.
Streamers: Black Double Bunnies #2-6, Woolly Bugger #2-6, JJ Special #2-6.

When to Fish:

The Flathead River fishes well in the spring and fall.

Seasons & Limits:

The standard fishing regulations for the *Western* fishing district apply. Please check the *Montana Fishing Regulations and Etiquette* section.

Exceptions to Standard Regulations
Confluence of the North and Middle Forks to Flathead Lake
  Combined Trout: 5 daily and in possession.
  Lake trout: 15 daily and in possession.
  Extended season for whitefish and lake trout, and catch-and-release for other game fish open December 1 through the third Saturday in May with artificial lures and/or maggots only.
  Catch-and-release for cutthroat trout.
Flathead Indian Reservation Boundary to mouth
  Open entire year.
  Northern pike: 5 daily and in possession, must be over 24 inches.

Nearby Fly Fishing:

Middle, North and South Forks of the Flathead, Clark Fork, Kootenai.

Accommodations & Services:

With the nearby towns of Kalispell, Polson, Dixon, and Bigfork there are several options for camping, lodging and dining. The Outlook Inn B & B (888-857-VIEW) offers an amazing setting overlooking Flathead Lake close to Kalispell.

Rating: 7

The lack of crowding, the stunning scenery, and the diversity of species in combination with eager fish, offset the lack of numbers and size of the trout.

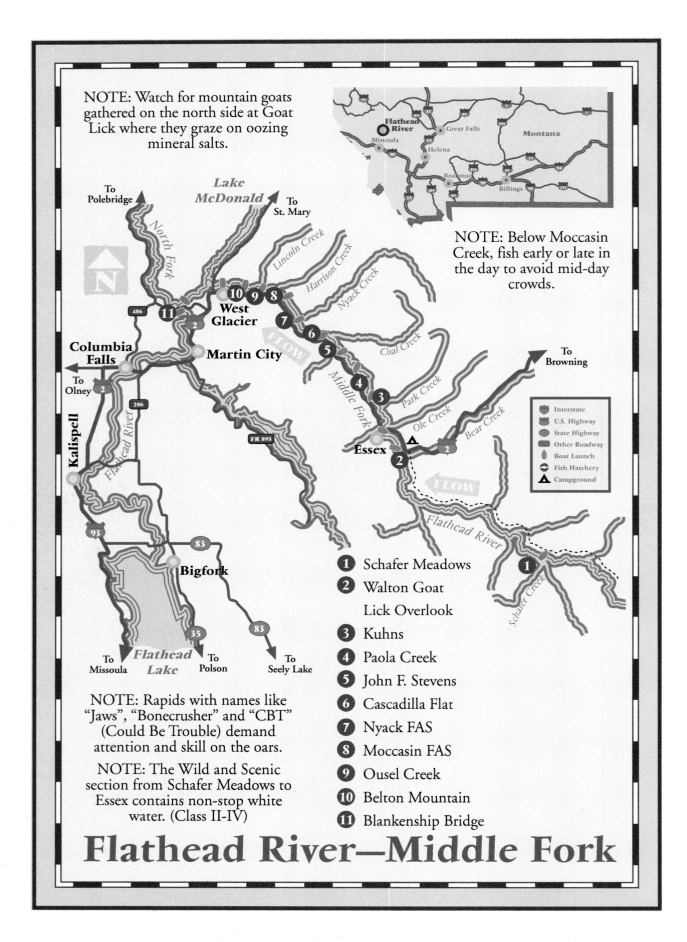

NOTE: Watch for mountain goats gathered on the north side at Goat Lick where they graze on oozing mineral salts.

NOTE: Below Moccasin Creek, fish early or late in the day to avoid mid-day crowds.

NOTE: Rapids with names like "Jaws", "Bonecrusher" and "CBT" (Could Be Trouble) demand attention and skill on the oars.

NOTE: The Wild and Scenic section from Schafer Meadows to Essex contains non-stop white water. (Class II-IV)

1 Schafer Meadows
2 Walton Goat Lick Overlook
3 Kuhns
4 Paola Creek
5 John F. Stevens
6 Cascadilla Flat
7 Nyack FAS
8 Moccasin FAS
9 Ousel Creek
10 Belton Mountain
11 Blankenship Bridge

Legend:
- Interstate
- U.S. Highway
- State Highway
- Other Roadway
- Boat Launch
- Fish Hatchery
- Campground

Flathead River—Middle Fork

Flathead River
Middle Fork

The Middle Fork of the Flathead enjoys the title of Montana's "Wildest River," due to its careening whitewater path through the Bob Marshall Wilderness, the Great Bear Wilderness and along the southwest border of Glacier National Park to its confluence with the North Fork of the Flathead. The 73-mile course of the Middle Fork plays host to 27 miles of 'Wild and Scenic' designated water with a healthy population of westslope cutthroat and a burgeoning population of rainbow trout.

The upper river at Schafer Meadows can be reached exclusively by foot, horseback or plane. The 'Wild and Scenic' stretch down to Essex contains non-stop whitewater from Type II to exhilarating Type IV. Portages may not be possible along the most difficult whitewater sections due to tight canyon walls and steep terrain. Additionally, the water may become too low to float by August, so check in at West Glacier for current river conditions. This float is for well-prepared experts only.

The river terminates its "Wild and Scenic," status at the town of Essex and thereafter is qualified as Recreational. The thirty miles from Essex to Moccasin Creek contains whitewater sections up to Type III and is still very hazardous due to tight

Types of Fish:
Rainbow, Bull, and Westslope Cutthroat Trout.

Known Hatches:
Year-round: Midges.
April-June: Baetis, Gray Drake.
June-August: Caddis, Gray Drake.
July: Salmonfly.
July-August: Hoppers, PMDs.
September-Early October: Hoppers, Baetis.

Equipment to Use:
Rods: 4-6 weight, 8-9 feet in length.
Lines: Weight forward floating for dry fly and nymph fishing.
Leaders: 9' 4-5x for dries, 7½' 4x for nymphing, and 4' 1x-2x for streamers.
Wading: Swift rapids make for harder wading. Chest-high waders suggested.

Flies to Use:
Dries: Griffith's Gnat #18-22, Blue Winged Olives #18-20, Parachute Adams #16-20, Caddis #14-18, Stimulator #8-12, Parachute Hopper #6-10, Royal Wulff #12-16, Royal Trude #12-16, Ant #14-16.
Nymphs: Brassie #18-24, Pheasant Tail Nymph #16-20, Kaufmann's Stone #2-8, Brown Rubber Legs #6-12, Serendipity #16-20, Sparkle Pupa #16-18, Beadhead Copper John #12-16, Lightning Bug #16-18.
Streamers: Woolly Bugger #2-8, JJ Special #2-8.

Evenings on the Middle Fork offer peace and solitude free from recreational raft traffic. Photo by Brian Grossenbacher.

Stunning vistas await around every turn of the Middle Fork.
Photo by Brian Grossenbacher.

corners and excessive logjams. Highway 2 parallels the Middle Fork from Essex to West Glacier, and access is readily available to those anglers willing to scramble down the steep rocky banks to the river. The cardinal rule of fishing applies—the more difficult the access, the better the fishing.

Downstream from Moccasin Creek the river receives intense pressure from whitewater recreationalists throughout the summer. The best fishing in this section is found early and late in the day in order to avoid midday crowds. From West Glacier to its confluence with the North Fork, the river widens and slows and is no longer a viable trout fishery.

Because of the fast heavy water on the Middle Fork, the fish have little time to inspect their next meal. Instead, they rise enthusiastically to reasonable presentations of buoyant attractor dries, and will aggressively feed on large nymphs and streamers.

The Middle Fork flows through prime grizzly habitat, and proper precautions should be taken when traveling in bear country. Additionally, the weather in the Glacier region can change dramatically, even in the heat of the summer. Before traveling into the Wilderness areas of the Middle Fork, make sure to be properly prepared for all weather and emergency conditions.

Large attractor dries work well on the fast, heavy water of the Middle Fork. Photo by Brian Grossenbacher.

When to Fish:
The Middle Fork of the Flathead River is best fished from early-July through early-September due to runoff early in the season and colder weather in fall.

Seasons & Limits:
The standard fishing regulations for the *Western* fishing district apply. Please check the *Montana Fishing Regulations and Etiquette* section.
Exceptions to Standard Regulations
All Streams within the Wilderness
   Combined Trout: 3 daily and in possession, none over 12 inches. Includes rainbow trout, cutthroat trout and grayling.
Non-Wilderness Portion
   Extended whitefish season and catch-and release for trout open December 1 to third Saturday in May with artificial lures and/or maggots only.
   Angling is closed within 100-yard radius of the Bear Creek stream mouth June 1 through August 31.
   Catch-and-release for cutthroat trout.
   Montana/Glacier National Park boundary is the ordinary high water mark on the park side of the river.

Nearby Fly Fishing:
South, North and Main stem of the Flathead, Kootenai, Hungry Horse Reservoir, Glacier National Park.

Accommodations & Services:
If staying near Essex, check out the famous Izzak Walton Inn (406-888-5700: www.izzakwaltoninn.com). In West Glacier there are countless lodging and camping options, either through Glacier National Park or private lodges. Check out www.montanascenicloop.com/lodging.html for a list of options.

Rating: 7
Another spectacular setting to wet a line. Access to the best fishing sections of the Middle Fork is a tad more formidable than that of the South Fork, plus the sections that are easily accessible are inundated by recreational floaters. Regardless, the Middle Fork offers eager trout willing to take a dry fly, and a beautiful setting.

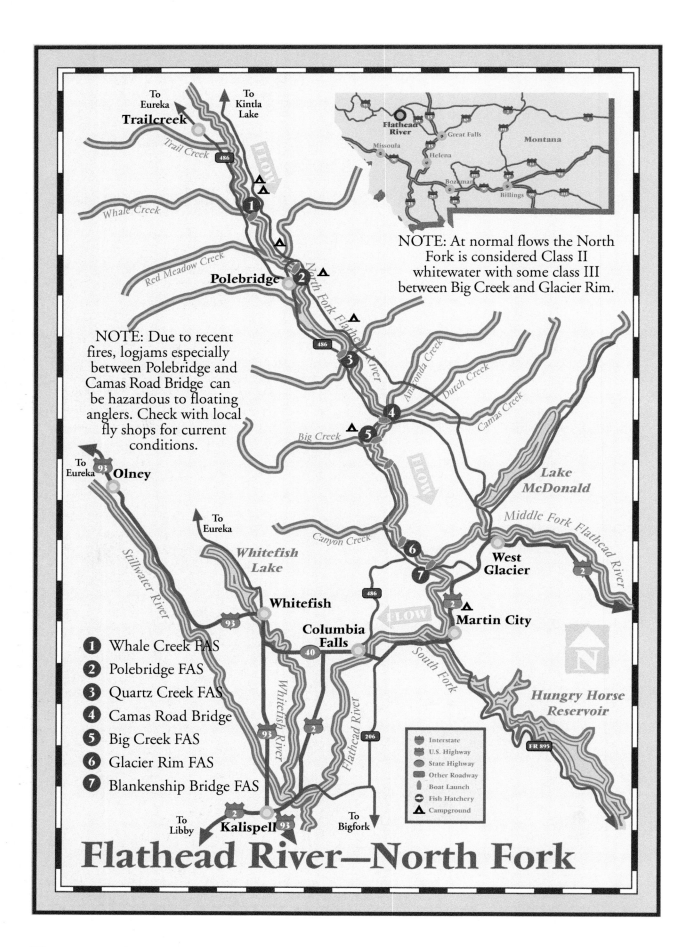

NOTE: At normal flows the North Fork is considered Class II whitewater with some class III between Big Creek and Glacier Rim.

NOTE: Due to recent fires, logjams especially between Polebridge and Camas Road Bridge can be hazardous to floating anglers. Check with local fly shops for current conditions.

1 Whale Creek FAS
2 Polebridge FAS
3 Quartz Creek FAS
4 Camas Road Bridge
5 Big Creek FAS
6 Glacier Rim FAS
7 Blankenship Bridge FAS

Interstate
U.S. Highway
State Highway
Other Roadway
Boat Launch
Fish Hatchery
Campground

Flathead River—North Fork

Flathead River
North Fork

The North Fork of the Flathead originates in British Columbia and flows south for 57 miles in Montana to the confluence of the Middle Fork just outside of West Glacier. The upper 42 miles in Montana is designated "Wild and Scenic," according to the National Wildlife and Scenic Rivers Act. The North Fork forms the western boundary of Glacier National Park, and provides anglers easy access, excellent scenery, and an unspoiled westslope cutthroat fishery. The cold clear waters of the North Fork are not high in nutrients and do not sustain a tremendous trout population by Montana standards, however there are certainly enough migrating westslope cutthroat, and occasional rainbow trout, to make the fishing entertaining, while taking in the overall experience of this spectacular riparian corridor.

The North Fork fish are not picky and typically can be caught with general attractor patterns such as the royal Wulff, parachute Adams, and PMX. Nymph fishing tandem rigs below strike indicators and streamer fishing with sink tip lines can bring up some bigger fish, but the overall average trout on the

Rainbow release. Photo by Brian Grossenbacher.

One can fish for westslope cutthroat the entire length of the North Fork in the U.S. and into Canada. Photo by Brian Grossenbacher.

Dense forests and steep banks make floating a good option on the North Fork. Photo by Jenny Grossenbacher.

North Fork is around 10"-12". Bull trout are present in the North Fork, but should not be fished for intentionally. If you do catch a bull trout, release it quickly to help preserve this threatened species.

Two roads parallel the North Fork—Highway 486 on the west side of the river and the North Fork Road on the east. These roads give anglers and recreationalists access at multiple sites on both sides of the river but also detract somewhat from the wilderness ambience. Due to the large size of the water, high, steep banks and densely-forested banks, float fishing is certainly the best mode for fishing the North Fork. At normal flows the North Fork is considered Class II whitewater suitable for novice floaters, with some class III whitewater (suitable for intermediates) between Big Creek and Glacier Rim.

Nathan Hadley releasing a nice rainbow.
Photo by Brian Grossenbacher.

Types of Fish:
Westslope Cutthroat, Rainbow and Bull Trout.

Known Hatches:
Year-round: Midges.
April-June: Baetis, Gray Drake.
June-August: Caddis, Gray Drake.
July: Salmonfly.
July-August: Hoppers, PMDs.
September-Early October: Hoppers, Baetis.

Equipment to Use:
Rods: 4-6 weight, 8-9 feet in length.
Lines: Weight forward floating line for dry fly and nymph fishing.
Leaders: 9' 4-5x for dries, 7½' 4x for nymphing, and 4' 1x-2x for streamers.
Wading: High, steep banks make for difficult access for waders. Float fishing is typically the best option. Chest-high waders suggested.

Flies to Use:
Dries: Griffith's Gnat #18-22, Blue Winged Olives #18-20, Parachute Adams #16-20, Caddis #14-18, Stimulator #8-12, Parachute Hopper #6-10, Royal Wulff #12-16, Royal Trude #12-16, Ant #14-16.
Nymphs: Brassie #18-24, Pheasant Tail Nymph #16-20, Kaufmann's Stone #2-8, Brown Rubber Legs #6-12, Serendipity #16-20, Sparkle Pupa #16-18, Beadhead Copper John #12-16, Lightning Bug #16-18.
Streamers: Woolly Bugger #2-8, JJ Special #2-8.

When to Fish:
The North Fork of the Flathead River is best fished in July and August when larger numbers of trout have migrated into the river.

Seasons & Limits:
The standard fishing regulations for the *Western* fishing district apply. Please check the *Montana Fishing Regulations and Etiquette* section.
Exceptions to Standard Regulations
Applies to entire water body:
  Catch-and-release for cutthroat trout.
  Extended season for whitefish and catch-and-release for trout open December 1 to third Saturday in May with artificial lures and/or maggots only.
  June 1 through August 31: Closed to angling within 100-yard radius of the Big Creek mouth.
  Montana/Glacier National Park boundary is the middle of the river.

Nearby Fly Fishing:
South, Middle and Main stem of the Flathead, Kootenai, Hungry Horse Reservoir, Glacier National Park.

Accommodations & Services:
Due to the close proximity to Glacier National Park and the Flathead National Forest, camping options abound. For lodging or cabin rentals check out West Glacier, in particular the Smokey Bear Ranch (800-555-3806: www.smokybear.com) or try the Polebridge Mercantile and Cabins in Polebridge (406-888-5105).

Rating: 6
Although scenic by anyone's standards, the North Fork offers fewer trout than the other Forks of the Flathead and more traffic, as the highway parallels the river for most of its length.

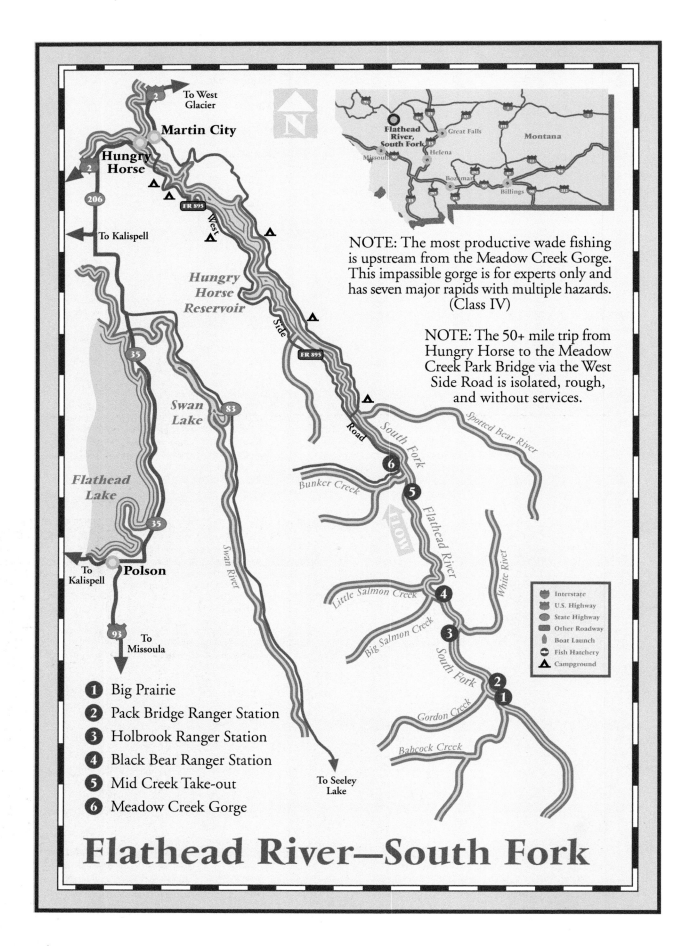

NOTE: The most productive wade fishing is upstream from the Meadow Creek Gorge. This impassible gorge is for experts only and has seven major rapids with multiple hazards. (Class IV)

NOTE: The 50+ mile trip from Hungry Horse to the Meadow Creek Park Bridge via the West Side Road is isolated, rough, and without services.

Legend:
- Interstate
- U.S. Highway
- State Highway
- Other Roadway
- Boat Launch
- Fish Hatchery
- Campground

1. Big Prairie
2. Pack Bridge Ranger Station
3. Holbrook Ranger Station
4. Black Bear Ranger Station
5. Mid Creek Take-out
6. Meadow Creek Gorge

Flathead River—South Fork

Flathead River
South Fork

As one of the last truly wild rivers in the lower 48, the South Fork of the Flathead offers anglers a unique backcountry fly-fishing experience. The South Fork begins in the heart of the Bob Marshall Wilderness at the confluence of Youngs and Danaher creeks and flows north for just over 100 miles to its confluence with the main fork of the Flathead at the town of Hungry Horse. Access to the South Fork is difficult from any direction. Whether by foot or by horse, the South Fork demands a considerable investment in time and energy before you wet a line.

Access to the upper river requires at least a 20-mile hike or horseback trip from Holland Lake or Seely Lake trailheads. This section down to the Spotted Bear River is designated "Wild and Scenic," according to the National Wild and Scenic Rivers Act. The entire section, with the exception of Meadow Creek Gorge, is straightforward wade fishing in gin clear water to an enthusiastic population of wild westslope cutthroat trout and Arctic grayling. The Meadow Creek Gorge is an extremely steep, narrow gorge that is virtually inaccessible by foot. The South Fork Trail parallels the rest of the river throughout this section, providing excellent foot access. Remember, this is prime grizzly habitat, follow all precautions when heading into bear country.

Types of Fish:
Bull & Westslope Cutthroat Trout, Arctic Grayling, Whitefish.

Known Hatches:
Year-round: Midges.
April-June: Baetis, Gray Drake.
June-August: Caddis, Gray Drake.
July: Salmonfly.
July-August: Hoppers, PMDs.
September-Early October: Hoppers, Baetis.

Equipment to Use:
Rods: 4-6 weight, 8-9 feet in length.
Lines: Weight forward floating line for dry fly and nymph fishing.
Leaders: 9' 4-5x for dries, 7½' 4x for nymphing, 4' 1x-2x for streamers.
Wading: Wading is relatively easy. Wet wading is an option during the warmer summer months, otherwise hip-high waders are suggested.

Flies to Use:
Dries: Griffith's Gnat #18-22, Blue Winged Olives #18-20, Parachute Adams #16-20, Caddis #14-18, Stimulator #8-12, Parachute Hopper #6-10, Royal Wulff #12-16, Royal Trude #12-16, Ant #14-16.
Nymphs: Brassie #18-24, Pheasant Tail Nymph #16-20, Kaufmann's Stone #2-8, Brown Rubber Legs #6-12, Serendipity #16-20, Sparkle Pupa #16-18, Beadhead Copper John #12-16, Lightning Bug #16-18.
Streamers: Woolly Bugger #2-8, JJ Special #2-10.

Fishing the green waters south of Hungry Horse.
Photo by Brian Grossenbacher.

Hooking a westslope cutthroat here just might attract a bull trout as well.

If you do not have several days to commit to backcountry travel, access to the river above Hungry Horse Reservoir can be gained via the West Reservoir Road from the town of Hungry Horse. This is a 50+ mile bumpy trip down an isolated dirt road to the Meadow Creek Pack Bridge. Allow up to four hours to make this drive. From here, anglers can pick up the South Fork Trail and have ready access to the river. The easiest and most productive wade fishing is found upstream of Meadow Creek Gorge.

The five miles of the South Fork below Hungry Horse dam is steadily improving, after a modification to the dam in the mid 1990s to allow water to be drawn from any level of the reservoir. Prior to this change, all water was drawn off the bottom of the reservoir, creating near freezing temperatures year-round. The shockingly-cold water negatively affected aquatic insects and trout both in the South Fork and the main stem of the Flathead below the confluence. Fishing continues to improve in this section with each passing season.

Due to the lack of pressure on the South Fork, the trout will rise readily to most attractor patterns. Caddis and mayfly patterns are common staples (sizes #12-16), and hoppers are very productive later in July and into August.

The South Fork of the Flathead is the only river in Montana where you can legally fish for bull trout, displayed here by Fred Deibel. Photo by Joe Dilshneider.

When to Fish:
The South Fork of the Flathead River is best fished from early July through early September.

Seasons & Limits:
The standard fishing regulations for the *Western* fishing district apply. Please check the *Montana Fishing Regulations and Etiquette* section.

Exceptions to Standard Regulations

All Waters Upstream from Hungry Horse Dam, including Hungry Horse Reservoir and Tributaries, except Meadow Creek Section (See below)

Combined Trout: 3 daily and in possession, no fish over 12 inches in rivers and streams. Includes rainbow trout, cutthroat trout and grayling.

Maintstream upstream from Hungry Horse Reservoir (from Crossover Boat Ramp south and upstream to the confluence of Youngs and Danaher creeks)

Bull trout: catch-and-release from the third Saturday in May through August 15. A Hungry Horse/South Fork Flathead Bull Trout Catch Card must be in possession when catch-and-release fishing for bull trout. See Special License requirements for application information. All bull trout must be released immediately. It is unlawful to possess a live bull trout for any reason.

Meadow Creek Bridge to Spotted Bear Foot Bridge and tributaries

Catch-and-release only.
Artificial lures only.

Hungry Horse Dam Downstream to Devil's Elbow and tributaries

Closed entire year.

Devil's Elbow Downstream to mouth and tributaries

Catch-and-release for cutthroat trout. Extended season for whitefish and catch-and-release for trout open December 1 to third Saturday in May with artificial lures and/or maggots only.

Nearby Fly Fishing:
Middle, North and Main stem of the Flathead, Kootenai, Hungry Horse Reservoir.

Accommodations & Services:
Check out the quaint Tamarack Lodge in the town of Hungry Horse (406-387-4420: www.historictamaracklodge.com). If you want the full experience of backcountry angling, try the Bob Marshall Wilderness Ranch (406-754-2285: www.wildernessranch.com) for a multi-day pack trip.

Rating: 8
For the sheer beauty and solitude of this *Wild and Scenic River* and the surrounding Bob Marshall Wilderness, this river should rank high atop any backcountry angler's list. Add to that the eagerness of the trout to take a dry, the lack of any road noise to disturb anglers or wildlife, and the only legal opportunity to fish for bull trout in a Montana river, and you have an amazing fishing experience. The lack of accessibility can be considered a plus or a minus depending on the judge.

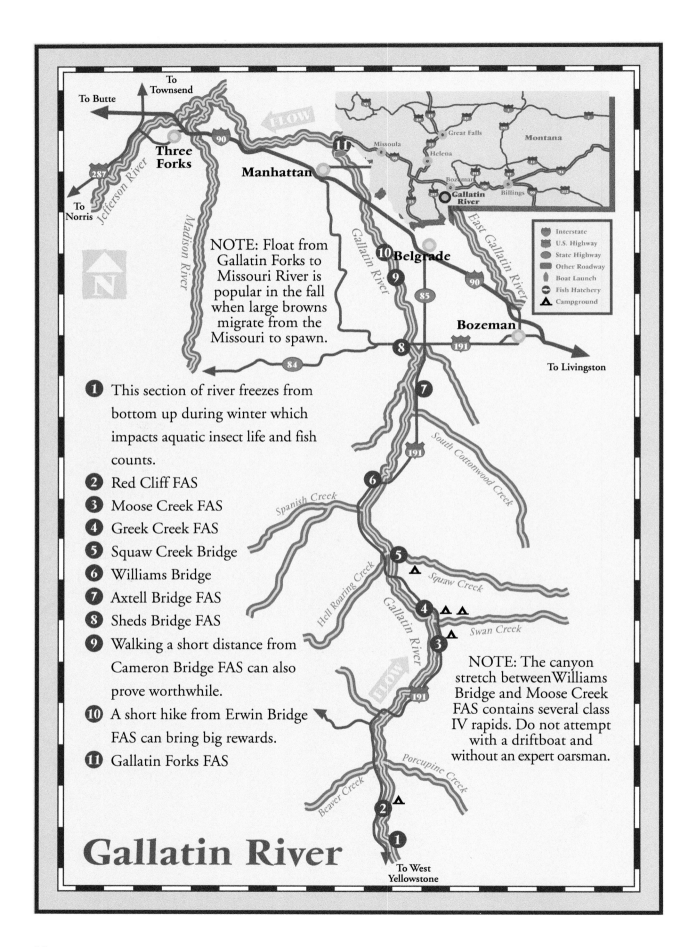

NOTE: Float from Gallatin Forks to Missouri River is popular in the fall when large browns migrate from the Missouri to spawn.

1. This section of river freezes from bottom up during winter which impacts aquatic insect life and fish counts.
2. Red Cliff FAS
3. Moose Creek FAS
4. Greek Creek FAS
5. Squaw Creek Bridge
6. Williams Bridge
7. Axtell Bridge FAS
8. Sheds Bridge FAS
9. Walking a short distance from Cameron Bridge FAS can also prove worthwhile.
10. A short hike from Erwin Bridge FAS can bring big rewards.
11. Gallatin Forks FAS

NOTE: The canyon stretch between Williams Bridge and Moose Creek FAS contains several class IV rapids. Do not attempt with a driftboat and without an expert oarsman.

Gallatin River

Gallatin River

Unbeknownst to most anglers, the Gallatin River served as the stunt double for the Big Blackfoot River during the filming of Norman MacLean's, *A River Runs Through It*. One of the three forks of the Missouri, the Gallatin was named after Albert Gallatin, the Secretary of the Treasury during the Lewis and Clark expedition. The Gallatin exits the northwestern corner of Yellowstone Park as a modest meadow stream and quickly gains steam as it heads towards Big Sky and the gradient and flow increases. Enhanced by tributaries such as Fan Creek, Specimen, and notably the Taylor's Fork, the Gallatin adopts a personality from each of its tributaries. Taylor's Fork plays the most colorful role as the villainous sediment-rich enemy of the Gallatin during run-off and after each summer rainstorm. The bentonite-rich soil of the Taylor drainage turns the Gallatin off color at the first sign of rain, and can keep the river unfishable for days afterward. Access along the Gallatin is excellent from Highway 191 throughout the canyon with plentiful pull-outs and moderately easy wading. Sections of the Gallatin between the Taylor's Fork and Big Sky freeze from the bottom up in the winter, and as a result, the aquatic insect life and fish counts are not as prolific as they are downstream. The straightforward nature of the Gallatin, with beautiful canyon walls and thick lodge pole stands, makes this a terrific option for the wading angler. Attractor dries and nymphs work best in the fast moving

Fisherman on the Gallatin River at Axtell Bridge.
Photo by Brian Grossenbacher.

Types of Fish:
Brown, Rainbow and Cutthroat Trout, Whitefish.

Known Hatches:
Year-round: Midges. Mid March-Late April: Baetis, Midges.
Late April-Mid May: Caddis.
June-July: Salmonflies, Golden Stones, Caddis, Green Drake, Caddis.
July-August: Spruce Moths, Yellow Sallies, Ants, Beetles, Hoppers, Caddis, Noctural Stones.
August-September: Spruce Moths, Mahogany Dun, Caddis.
September-October: Baetis.

Equipment to Use:
Rods: 4-5 weight, 8-9 feet in length.
Lines: Floating line for dries & nymphs, sink tip for streamers.
Leaders: 7½' 3x for nymphs, 9' 4-6x for dries, 7' 0-2x for streamers.
Wading: Wading can be tricky due to swift currents. Because of deeper runs and pools, wear full waders and wading belt except during the warmest days.

Flies to Use:
Dries: Parachute Adams #16-22, BWO #18-20, Goddard's Caddis #14-18, Elk Hair Caddis #12-18, PMX #8-12, Rusty Spinner #14-16, Royal Wulff #12-16, Royal Trude #12-18, Speckled X #12.
Nymphs: Hare's Ear #8-18, Sparkle Pupa #18-20, Copper John #12-18, Green & Brown Bugger #6-8, Prince Nymph #12-16, Pheasant Tail #16-20, Lightning Bug #14-18, Serendipity #14-18, Ugly Prince #4-8, Bitch Creek #4-8, Girdle Bug #4-8, Anderson's Brown Stone #6-8.
Streamers: Green or Brown Bugger #2-6.

When to Fish:
The Gallatin is one of the best year-round rivers in Montana. February and March offer exceptional fishing with midges and nymphs. With spring comes solid baetis and caddis fishing. All summer long attractor patterns and hoppers keep the dry fly fisherman content. Autumn brings the baetis back again, as well as solid streamer fishing. Nymph fishermen can stay busy year-round with any attractor nymph.

Seasons & Limits:
The standard fishing regulations for the *Central* and *National Park Service* fishing districts apply. Please check the *Montana Fishing Regulations and Etiquette* section.
Exceptions to Standard Regulations
Entire River
   Open entire year.
Yellowstone National Park to East Gallatin River
   Closed to fishing from boats.

Nearby Fly Fishing:
Lower & Upper Madison, East, North & West Forks of the Gallatin, Yellowstone, Paradise Valley Spring Creeks, Missouri, Yellowstone National Park, Hyalite Reservoir.

Jenny enjoys the fruits of year round fishing on the canyon stretch of the Gallatin.
Photo by Brian Grossenbacher.

canyon section, as the fish don't have long to think about their feeding opportunities.

As the Gallatin exits the canyon the valley opens and the river broadens accordingly. The fish increase slightly in size and browns increase in number. Access is good from Williams, Axtell, Shed's and Cameron Bridges respectively, and the fishing gets exponentially better the greater distance you hike from the bridges in either direction. Hoppers rule the roost in the summer months, and larger stone fly patterns with a beadhead dropper are successful year-round.

Downstream from Shed's Bridge the river braids and is further divided by irrigation diversions that seriously deplete the Lower Gallatin in the summer months. Below Manhattan and the convergence of the East Gallatin, anglers can float the Gallatin (when flows allow) down to the Headwaters State Park and the confluence with the Missouri. This is a popular float in the fall when large spawning browns migrate upstream from the Missouri.

Attractor dries & nymphs work well in the fast moving water of the Gallatin. Photo by Brian Grossenbacher.

Accommodations & Services:

Bozeman is a 10-minute drive and offers many lodging options. Below are a few of our favorites: The Gallatin Gateway Inn (800-676-3522: www.gallatingatewayinn. com) was built in 1927 as a stopping point for the Chicago/Milwaukee railroad. This historically-restored inn just south of Bozeman, offers a five-star restaurant, cigar-friendly bar, incomparable atmosphere, and comfortable rooms.

For a vacation home, try Mountain Home Vacation Rentals (800-550-4589: www.mountain-home.com). If you want a B&B and are planning to fish the Yellowstone River as well, check out Howler's Inn (406-586-0304: www.howlersinn.com). Howler's offers a quaint country setting halfway between Bozeman and Livingston. For camping there are several Forest Service campgrounds along the river, especially farther up (south) the Canyon. Some of our favorites are Squaw Creek, Swan Creek and Red Cliff.

Bozeman has the best restaurant selection around for a town its size. Montana Ale Works is a local favorite downtown on Main Street. They offer a full bar and a tasty and varied menu. An unexpected find on Main Street is Plunk, a wonderfully quaint, yet hip wine bar with an excellent chef. A client favorite for higher-end dining is Boodles on Main Street with live jazz on the weekends and a great chef. For a great martini, cigar, and a trout appetizer try the Mint on Main Street in Belgrade. BBQ? Tromp on over to Bar 3 BBQ, also in Belgrade. For pizza, try MacKenzie River Pizza downtown on Main Street. If you aren't in a hurry, go sit on the patio of The Garage and sip a cold one while waiting on a great burger, grilled salmon or salad.

Coffee shops are on just about every block. The Community Co-Op on Main Street offers organic coffees and teas and wireless Internet. Any of the Rocky Mountain Roasting Company shops offer excellent coffee and free wireless. For a great breakfast or lunch, try the Community Co-Op, Main Street Over Easy, the Cat Eye Café or the epic breakfast burrito at Soby's in the old Bozeman Hotel.

Rating: 9

The Gallatin's year-round fishability, great access, beautiful scenery, and healthy wild trout population make for a classic and memorable wade-fishing experience.

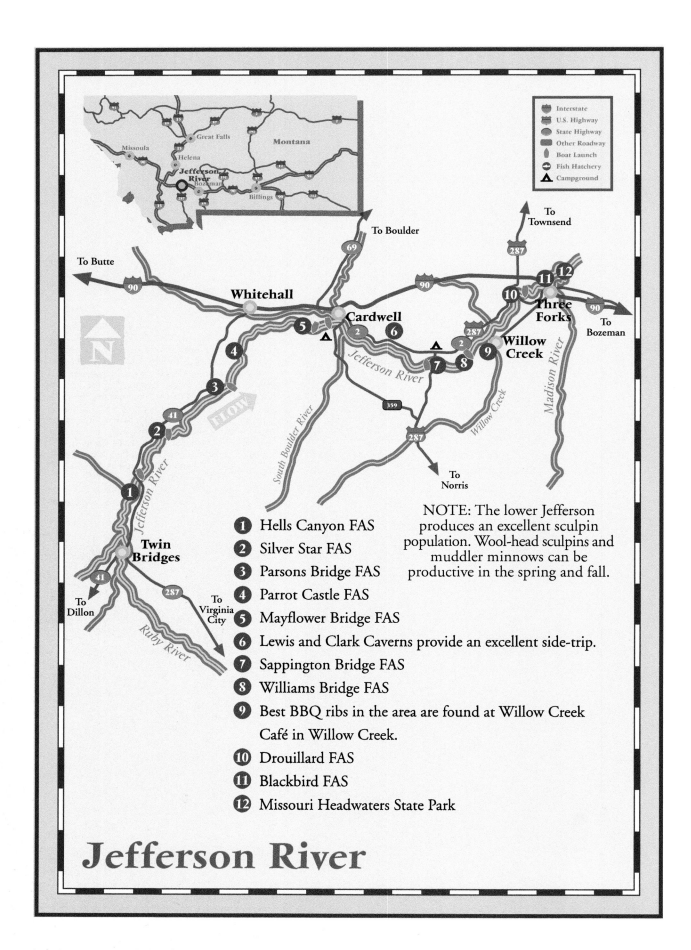

Legend:
- Interstate
- U.S. Highway
- State Highway
- Other Roadway
- Boat Launch
- Fish Hatchery
- Campground

Montana

Missoula
Great Falls
Helena
Jefferson River
Bozeman
Billings

To Boulder
To Townsend
To Butte
To Bozeman
To Dillon
To Virginia City
To Norris

Whitehall
Cardwell
Three Forks
Willow Creek
Twin Bridges

Jefferson River
South Boulder River
Willow Creek
Madison River
Ruby River

FLOW

1. Hells Canyon FAS
2. Silver Star FAS
3. Parsons Bridge FAS
4. Parrot Castle FAS
5. Mayflower Bridge FAS
6. Lewis and Clark Caverns provide an excellent side-trip.
7. Sappington Bridge FAS
8. Williams Bridge FAS
9. Best BBQ ribs in the area are found at Willow Creek Café in Willow Creek.
10. Drouillard FAS
11. Blackbird FAS
12. Missouri Headwaters State Park

NOTE: The lower Jefferson produces an excellent sculpin population. Wool-head sculpins and muddler minnows can be productive in the spring and fall.

Jefferson River

Jefferson River

The three forks of the Missouri were named after members of Thomas Jefferson's cabinet during the Lewis and Clark expedition. Ironically, it is the president's namesake river that has fallen the greatest distance from grace since that time.

The prolific practice of irrigation and diversion has all but sucked the life out of the Jefferson for most of its length. The Jefferson enjoys a Blue Ribbon pedigree as the offspring of the Big Hole, Beaverhead and Ruby rivers. This rich heritage however, cannot overcome the deficit water management practices that put the "Jeff" on the ropes every summer. As a result the river suffers from high temps, low oxygen, low water, and siltation.

Strangely enough fish do still populate the Jefferson, just not in great numbers. As you might expect, the time to fish the Jefferson is in the spring and fall when temperatures are cool and water levels are stable.

The Jefferson produces a strong population of sculpin and other bait fish. Therefore, you may want to employ a "chuck and duck," streamer strategy when fishing the Jefferson. If you are not a die-hard streamer fisherman, you may want to try dead drifting various crayfish patterns on the lower river.

Types of Fish:
Brown and Rainbow Trout, Whitefish.

Known Hatches:
Year-round: Midges.
Mid March-Late April: Baetis.
Late April-Mid July: Caddis.
Late June-July: PMDs, Caddis, Golden Stone, Yellow Sallies, Hoppers, Ants, Beetles.
September-Mid October: Tricos, Baetis.

Equipment to Use:
Rods: 4-6 weight, 8½-9 feet in length.
Lines: Floating line for dries and nymphs, sink tip for streamers.
Leaders: 9' 4-6x for dries, 7½' 3x-4x for nymphs, 7' 0-2x for streamers.
Wading: Best fished by a drift boat, however there is reasonable wading in low-water situations.

Flies to Use:
Dries: Parachute Adams #12-22, BWO #18-22, Goddard's Caddis #14-18, Elk Hair Caddis #14-18, Trico #18-22, Stimulator #8-16, Royal Wulff #12-16, Rusty Spinner #16-18, Griffith's Gnat #18-24, PMX #8-12, Parachute Hopper #6-10, Rogue Hopper #6-10.
Nymphs: Hare's Ear #12-20, Sparkle Pupa #18-20, Copper John #12-18, Green & Brown Bugger #2-6, Prince Nymph #12-16, Pheasant Tail #16-20, Lightning Bug #14-18, Serendipity #14-18, Red San Juan Worm #6-8, Kaufmann's Gold Stone #8-16.
Streamers: Black Crystal Bugger #2-6, Green, Brown, Black or Light-Olive Bugger #2-6, Clouser or Muddler Minnow #2-6, JJ Special #2-8, Sculpin #2-8, Leeches #2-8, Green, White or Natural Zonkers #2-6.

A healthy population of sculpin and crayfish create excellent streamer fishing on the Jefferson. Photo by Brian Grossenbacher.

The blending of two worlds… farmers and anglers alike enjoy the amazing Montana vistas. Photo by Jenny Grossenbacher.

The Jefferson begins its course at the confluence of the Beaverhead and Big Hole rivers just north of Twin Bridges. The Jefferson flows through agricultural pastureland for its first fifty miles at a moderate pace. Below Cardwell, the river then enters the Jefferson Canyon with steep walls and deep pools ideal for swimming on hot summer days. Access is good throughout this section via a set of railroad tracks on one side and road access on the other. Around Sappington Bridge the Jefferson opens into another wide agricultural valley as it braids and twists through cottonwood banks until its convergence with the Missouri. Look to the Jefferson as a journey of solitude in search of a few trout and you may find success…you will certainly find solitude.

Tributary enhancements and efforts to increase water flow are producing a gradual recovery of rainbows and browns.
Photo by Brian Grossenbacher.

When to Fish:

Spring and early summer can produce solid fishing opportunities. Late fall, end of September and October, is a great time to fish streamers for big trout. Avoid August on the lower river and, depending on the conditions, maybe even late-July through mid-September. The stream has frequent closures due to low-water conditions.

Seasons & Limits:

The standard fishing regulations for the *Central* fishing district apply. Please check the *Montana Fishing Regulations and Etiquette* section.

Exceptions to Standard Regulations

Entire River

   Open entire year.

Confluence of Beaverhead and Big Hole Rivers to Williams Bridge FAS

   Combined Trout: 3 brown trout daily and in possession, only 1 over 18 inches. Catch-and-release for rainbow trout.

Williams Bridge FAS to confluence with Missouri River

   Combined Trout: 5 brown trout daily and in possession, only 1 over 18 inches. Catch-and-release for rainbow trout.

Seasonal spawning closure at tributary mouths: Hells Canyon Creek and Willow Springs Creek

   Closed to fishing 100 yards upstream and downstream from the creek mouths from April 1 through April 30 and from October 15 through November 30.

Nearby Fly Fishing:

Madison, Beaverhead, Big Hole, Ruby, Willow Creek.

Accommodations & Services:

In Three Forks your best bet for lodging is the enchanting Sacajawea Hotel (406-285-6515: www.sacajaweahotel.com). It's only a five-minute jaunt to the tiny town of Willow Creek for world-class ribs. If you are fishing other rivers to the east consider staying in Bozeman (see the Lower Madison or Gallatin sidebars). If fishing farther west, look at the Big Hole or Beaverhead options. Wherever you stay, the Lewis & Clark Caverns outside of Three Forks are worth a visit.

Rating: 7.5 in late fall, 6 the rest of year.

For all the surrounding rivers of fame and the pure beauty of the Jefferson, one would certainly expect it to be another great Montana trout stream. Unfortunately, the pressures of over-irrigation have taken a toll on the river, and it is frequently under restrictions during late summer. When you hit the Jefferson at the right time (late fall), some large rainbows and browns can be found. We've heard reports of 5+ lb fish with regular catches of 20"+ trout. Keep in mind, there are approximately 200 trout/mile on the Jefferson, versus a couple of thousand/mile on some of Montana's best rivers. Regardless, one can expect a beautiful float, an abundance of wildlife, and few if any other anglers in sight on a float down the Jefferson. Those features alone are worth their weight in gold.

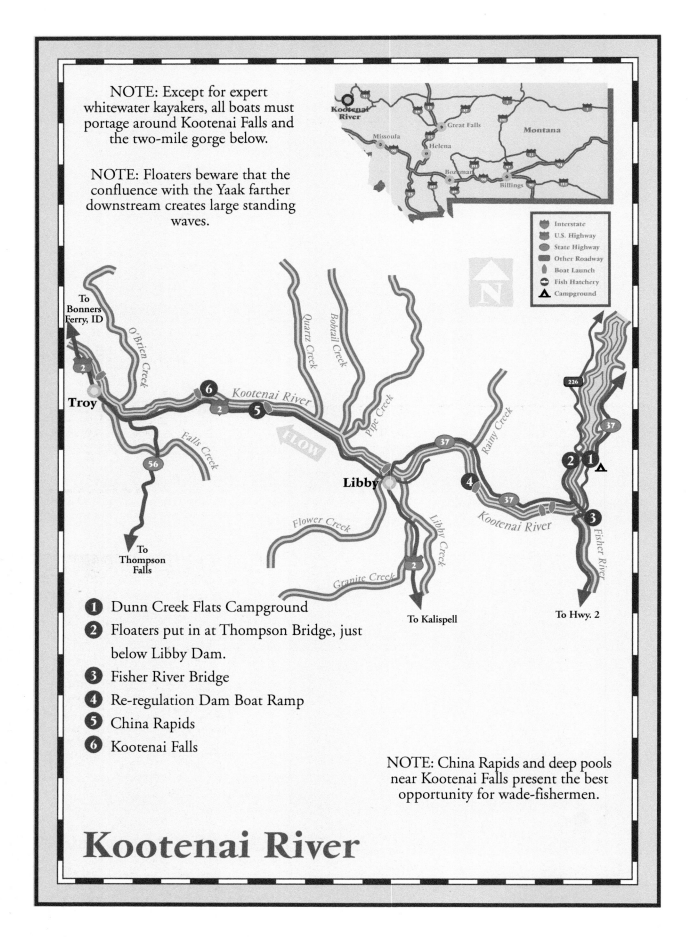

NOTE: Except for expert whitewater kayakers, all boats must portage around Kootenai Falls and the two-mile gorge below.

NOTE: Floaters beware that the confluence with the Yaak farther downstream creates large standing waves.

Interstate
U.S. Highway
State Highway
Other Roadway
Boat Launch
Fish Hatchery
Campground

To Bonners Ferry, ID

O'Brien Creek

Troy

Quartz Creek

Bobtail Creek

Kootenai River

Pipe Creek

Rainy Creek

226

37

FLOW

Falls Creek

56

Libby

37

2 1

4

37

Kootenai River

3

Fisher River

To Thompson Falls

Flower Creek

Libby Creek

Granite Creek

2

To Kalispell

To Hwy. 2

1 Dunn Creek Flats Campground
2 Floaters put in at Thompson Bridge, just below Libby Dam.
3 Fisher River Bridge
4 Re-regulation Dam Boat Ramp
5 China Rapids
6 Kootenai Falls

NOTE: China Rapids and deep pools near Kootenai Falls present the best opportunity for wade-fishermen.

Kootenai River

Kootenai River

The Kootenai is perhaps Montana's best Blue Ribbon secret, and due to its distant location in the extreme northwest corner of the state, it is likely to stay that way. Even by western standards, the Kootenai is a large river. Low flows on the Kootenai regularly exceed the Madison River at peak runoff. The river takes it name from the Kootenai Indians who fished and hunted this region 3,000 years before the first white settlers arrived. The Kootenai flows through the shadows of the Cabinet Mountains to the south and the majestic Purcell Mountain Range to the north. The limited fishing pressure, exceptional dry fly fishing and spectacular scenery, make a trip to the "Koot," worthy of venturing off the beaten path.

The river originates in British Columbia and flows through Montana for more than 100 miles, 50 of those miles however are submerged below the Lake Koocanusa formed in 1973 upon completion of the Libby Dam. The dam was built for hydroelectric power, and until recent years, flows would fluctuate wildly to meet electrical demand. Today, thanks to the hard work of the local Kootenai Valley Trout Unlimited Chapter, and local guides and anglers, the Kootenai flow regimes essentially mimic the natural hydrograph with big, spring run-off flows in May and early June then tapering down to very fishable flows around the middle of June-first of July depending on the yearly snowpack. The Kootenai may still fluctuate from December to March as flood control and power generation needs are met. Throughout the year anglers can always call the Libby Dam for a daily flow update at 406-293-3421. Wade fishing is best between 8,000 and 12,000 cfs.

Types of Fish:
Rainbow, Westslope Cutthroat, Bull, and Columbia Redband Trout, Whitefish.

Known Hatches:
Year-round: Midges.
Mid March-June: Baetis.
June-Early September: PMDs.
June-September: Caddis.
July-August: Green Drakes.

Equipment to Use:
Rods: 5-8 weight, 8½-9 feet in length.
Lines: Weight forward floating for dry fly and nymph fishing, high-density sinking tips and/or full sinking shooting heads for streamers.
Leaders: 9' 4x to 10' 6x for dry and nymphing, 4' 0x-2x for streamers.
Wading: Due to the size and the depth of the river, it is best fished from a boat. Where depth allows, wading is easy. Chest-high waders and wading belt are recommended.

Flies to Use:
Dries: Griffith's Gnat #18-22, Parachute Adams #16-20, Blue Winged Olives #18-20, PMD Sparkle Dun #16, X Caddis #14-18, Elk Hair Caddis #14-18, Parachute Hopper #10, Ant #14-16, Royal Wulff #14.
(Continued)

Mackenzie Grossenbacher below Kootenai Falls.
Photo by Jenny Grossenbacher.

The deep pools below Kootenai Falls make for excellent holding water for trout.

Unlike most rivers in Montana, the Kootenai is virtually drought resistant. There are no major irrigation diversions, and the generous snowfall in that region typically keeps the Koocanusa reservoir full to its banks. Also unique, the Kootenai and its tributaries are the only waters in Montana to contain a native strain of Columbia Redband trout. These football shaped rainbows are acrobatic and tenacious fighters.

The Upper Kootenai from the dam to Libby is 17 miles long and has excellent access along Mt. Hwy 37 and River Road. Floaters can put in at Thompson Bridge just a few hundred yards below the dam. Although there are some braided channels the main channel is large and a difficult river to read with some holes approaching 20 feet in depth. Look for seams and deeper pools, and any breaks in the current from inlet streams and other structure. The size of the Kootenai can be intimidating if you try to fish it bank to bank. Instead, look for the subtle breaks in the current, and concentrate your efforts on these structural "hot" zones.

The Kootenai made fishing headlines in 1997 when a state record 33-pound rainbow was caught just below the Libby Dam. To catch one of these monsters, consider using fast sinking lines with 7-9 weight rods and large streamers stripped erratically to mimic wounded baitfish that are regularly churned out of the turbines. Not to downplay the opportunity for a trophy class fish, the real draw of the Kootenai is the quality dry fly fishing to fish in the 12"-16" inch class. Although these fish do not receive as much pressure as in other parts of the state, they are by no means pushovers. Match the hatches accurately, and keep your flies in the feeding lanes of rising trout. These fish are stingy with their energy and will not move far to eat your fly. If you are not having luck, consider lengthening your leader and lightening your tippet.

Downstream from Libby, access is more difficult along US 2. The best access and the best fishing opportunities reside at China Rapids, and at Kootenai Falls. Large rocks and deep pools provide excellent holding water for trout. A swinging footbridge above the Kootenai Falls will bring you face to face to the stunning display of the falls. All boats with the exception of expert whitewater kayakers must portage Kootenai Falls and the two mile gorge below.

Below the river gorge, access is again available above and below the town of Troy, and again at the Yaak River campground. Floaters beware that the confluence of the Yaak River creates large standing waves. Inexperienced boaters should portage or pull out at above the confluence. Alert management and slot limits have improved the fishing on the Lower Kootenai markedly in the past several years. Trout numbers and sizes are on the rise. If you want an enjoyable and peaceful float with a few fish in between, this is certainly the stretch for you.

Overall, the quality fishing experience found on the Kootenai is markedly enhanced by the spectacular scenery and lack of fishing pressure. The Kootenai is a big and difficult river to read. Like a Zen koan (riddle) it reveals itself sparingly and only after careful study. Anglers may find their first experience on the Kootenai greatly enhanced by hiring a local guide.

Flies to Use: (Continued)

Nymphs: Lime Green Midge #20-22, Brassie #18-24, Tunghead Midge Pupa #18-22, Tunghead Prince Nymph #14, Brown Tunghead Stonefly Nymph #14, Pheasant Tail Nymph #16-20, Beadhead Copper John #16, Lightning Bug #16-18.
Streamers: Black/White Double Bunnies #2-6, Woolly Bugger #2-8, JJ Special #2-6.

When to Fish:

The Kootenai is a great dry fly river, offering dry fly fishing 75% of the season. Early- to mid-July will find you surrounded by heavy hatches of PMDs, Caddis, and Green Drakes. If you enjoy the cool, crisp days of autumn, the middle of September offers great terrestrial action. If you stick around long enough, by late September the river really turns on with big streamer action.

Seasons & Limits:

The standard fishing regulations for the *Western* fishing district apply. Please check the *Montana Fishing Regulations and Etiquette* section.
Exceptions to Standard Regulations
Libby Dam to Highway 37 Bridge (Near Fisher River)
    Open June 1 through March 31.
    Combined Trout: 4 daily and in possession, includes 3 under 13 inches and 1 over 24 inches.
Highway 37 Bridge (Near Fisher River) to Idaho Border
    Combined Trout: 4 daily and in possession, includes 3 under 13 inches and 1 over 18 inches.
    Open entire year.
Kootenai Falls to 0.8 Miles Downstream of Swinging Bridge
    Snagging: open for salmon from September 15 through November 30.

Nearby Fly Fishing:

Clark Fork, Yaak.

Accommodations & Services:

Just about anyone who enjoys fly fishing has heard of Tim Linehan. Tim's show with Trout Unlimited has brought a new side to fishing TV—one focused upon conservation and appreciation of the resource. Linehan Outfitting Company (800-596-0034: www. fishmontana.com) offers elegant, self-catered, log cabins located in Yaak or riverside accommodations at their Kootenai River House. The Kootenai house sleeps eight people, offers optional full service, and trout are outside the front door.

Rating: 9

Unlike many tailwater fisheries, where good fishing tapers off a few miles below the dam, the Kootenai fishes extremely well throughout its entire run from the Libby Dam to the Idaho border. It is a big, broad, uncrowded river surrounded by mountains covered with verdant coniferous forests. The Kootenai offers knee-deep, easy wading, coupled with scenic floating, and frequent catches of 12"-16" rainbows and cutthroats.

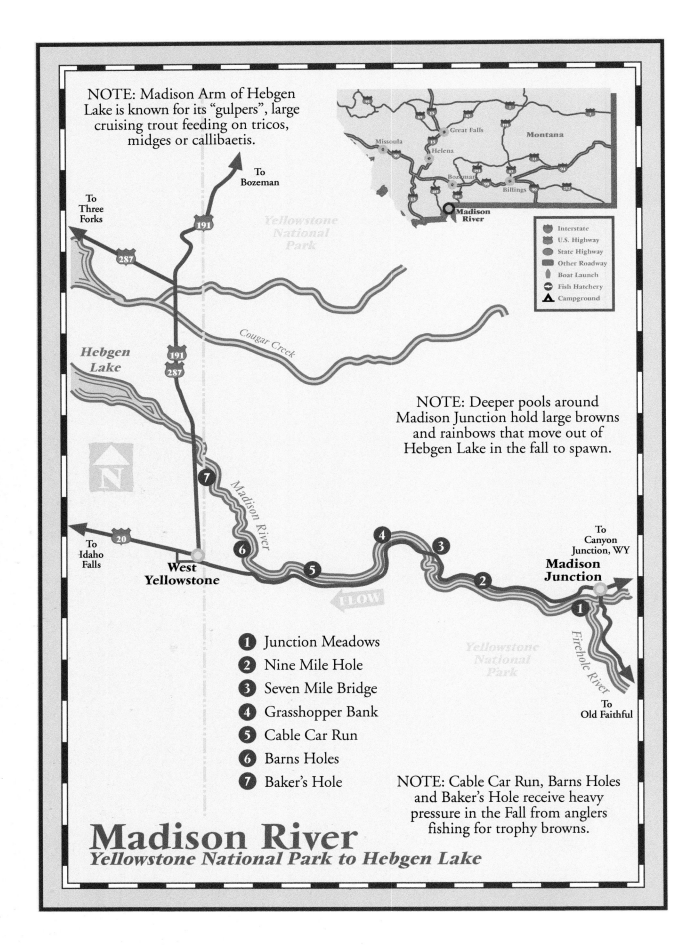

NOTE: Madison Arm of Hebgen Lake is known for its "gulpers", large cruising trout feeding on tricos, midges or callibaetis.

To Bozeman

To Three Forks

191

287

Yellowstone National Park

Montana

Missoula
Great Falls
Helena
Bozeman
Billings
Madison River

Interstate
U.S. Highway
State Highway
Other Roadway
Boat Launch
Fish Hatchery
Campground

Cougar Creek

Hebgen Lake

191
287

NOTE: Deeper pools around Madison Junction hold large browns and rainbows that move out of Hebgen Lake in the fall to spawn.

N

7

Madison River

To Idaho Falls

20

West Yellowstone

6

5

4

3

2

To Canyon Junction, WY

Madison Junction

1

FLOW

Yellowstone National Park

Firehole River

1 Junction Meadows
2 Nine Mile Hole
3 Seven Mile Bridge
4 Grasshopper Bank
5 Cable Car Run
6 Barns Holes
7 Baker's Hole

To Old Faithful

NOTE: Cable Car Run, Barns Holes and Baker's Hole receive heavy pressure in the Fall from anglers fishing for trophy browns.

Madison River
Yellowstone National Park to Hebgen Lake

Madison River
Yellowstone National Park to Hebgen Lake

The Madison River originates at the junction of the Firehole and Gibbon rivers in the northwestern corner of Yellowstone Park. Its modest beginnings as a meandering meadow stream underscore the fact that its 130-mile path to the Three Forks of the Missouri is a marathon, not a sprint. The upper reaches of the Madison in the park are best fished spring, early summer, and fall as the high temperatures of mid-summer are compounded by the multiple thermal features of the Firehole.

The Madison River in the Park enjoys a fall migratory run of spawning browns, and opportunistic rainbows that feed on wayward eggs. Anglers travel globally to take advantage of this fall run, and multitudes of trophy class trout are caught and released each season. Most anglers concentrate on the Cable Car Run, Barns Holes, and Baker's hole, but the fish can be found in virtually any deep run between Hebgen Lake and Madison Junction. Fishing the established "holes" on the Madison

Types of Fish:
Brown and Rainbow Trout, Whitefish.

Known Hatches:
Mid May-June: Baetis, PMDs, Caddis, Salmonflies.
Late June-July: Hoppers, Ants, Beetles.
September-Early November: Baetis, Streamers.

Equipment to Use:
Rods: 5-6 weight, 8½-9 feet in length.
Lines: Floating line for dries and nymphs.
Leaders: 7½' 4-5x for nymphs, 9' 5-x for dries, 7' 0-2x for streamers.
Wading: Easy wading due to flat bottom. Hip-high waders suggested.

Flies to Use:
Dries: Parachute Adams #12-22, BWO #18-22, Goddard's Caddis #14-18, Elk Hair Caddis #14-18, Rusty Spinner #16-18, PMX #8-12, Parachute Hopper #6-10.
Nymphs: Red San Juan Worm #6-8, Hare's Ear #12-20, Sparkle Pupa #18-20, Serendipity #14-18, Copper John #12-18, Green & Brown Bugger #4-6, Prince Nymph #8-16, Pheasant Tail #16-20, Lightning Bug #14-18.
Streamers: Green or Brown Bugger #2-6, White, Copper, Natural and Green Zonker #2-6.

Friendly visits and fishing advice are common from the YNP Rangers.
Photo by Jenny Grossenbacher.

The upper Madison near the Park offers stunning vistas.
Photo by Jenny Grossenbacher.

requires patience, adherence to the adopted etiquette, and a social appreciation for other anglers. Anglers typically fish the holes from top to bottom from one side of the river (typically south). After a few casts are made, a few steps are taken downstream. This rotation through the run ensures that everyone gets a fair shot. To enter the rotation, wait at the top of the run until a spot opens up. Successful techniques for this fall run range from stripping streamers, dead-drifting eggs and San Juan Worms, to swinging soft hackles.

For the vast majority of this stretch you'll need to purchase a Yellowstone National Park fishing license. They can be acquired at any local fly shop or just inside the park border at the ranger station.

Enough said.
Photo by Jenny Grossenbacher.

When to Fish:

This stretch of the Madison is fished best in Spring (opening day is the 3rd weekend in May) and early Summer, and then again in Fall until closing day, the first Saturday in November. The warmer temperatures of summer, coupled with the multiple-thermal features of the Firehole, effectively slow down the fishing from mid-July through August. The upper section is famous for the large browns that migrate out of Hebgen Lake for the spawn in late autumn.

Seasons & Limits:

The standard fishing regulations for the *Central* and *National Park Service* fishing districts apply. Please check the *Montana Fishing Regulations and Etiquette* section.
Exceptions to Standard Regulations
Yellowstone National Park Boundary to Hebgen Reservoir
　Combined Trout: 5 brown trout daily and in possession, only 1 over 18 inches. Catch-and-release for rainbow trout, except anglers 14 years of age and younger may take 1 rainbow trout daily and in possession, any size.
Hebgen Dam to Quake Lake
　Open entire year.

Nearby Fly Fishing:

Yellowstone National Park, Gallatin, Upper Madison, Ruby, Hebgen Lake, Cliff & Wade Lake.

Accommodations & Services:

West Yellowstone offers several hotels and lodges for varied tastes, including the wonderful getaway at the Firehole Ranch (406-646-7294: www.fireholeranch. com). Farther downstream check out The Old Kirby Place (888-875-8027: www.oldkirbyplace.com) or the West Fork Cabins (866-343-8267: www.wfork.com) which offer both cabins, RV spots and camping. For campers, there are numerous options within Yellowstone National Park and at Hebgen, Cliff, and Wade Lake, as well as countless Forest Service campgrounds around the area.

Rating: 9

Huge browns, beautiful setting, serious fishing. The one drawback is that this stretch is typically crowded, due to its popularity worldwide.

Late spring fishing surrounded by bison. Photo by Jenny Grossenbacher.

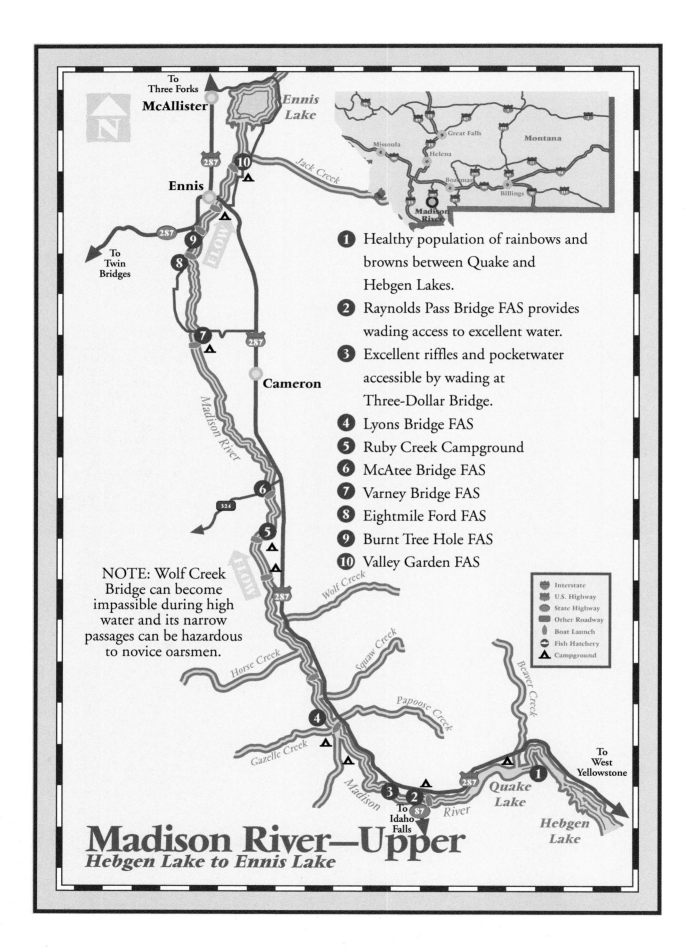

To
Three Forks

McAllister

Ennis Lake

Ennis

10

9

8

To
Twin
Bridges

7

287

Jack Creek

Madison River

Cameron

6

324

5

NOTE: Wolf Creek
Bridge can become
impassible during high
water and its narrow
passages can be hazardous
to novice oarsmen.

FLOW

287

Wolf Creek

Montana

Missoula

Great Falls

Helena

Bozeman

Billings

**Madison
River**

1. Healthy population of rainbows and browns between Quake and Hebgen Lakes.
2. Raynolds Pass Bridge FAS provides wading access to excellent water.
3. Excellent riffles and pocketwater accessible by wading at Three-Dollar Bridge.
4. Lyons Bridge FAS
5. Ruby Creek Campground
6. McAtee Bridge FAS
7. Varney Bridge FAS
8. Eightmile Ford FAS
9. Burnt Tree Hole FAS
10. Valley Garden FAS

Squaw Creek

Papoose Creek

Horse Creek

Beaver Creek

Interstate
U.S. Highway
State Highway
Other Roadway
Boat Launch
Fish Hatchery
Campground

4

Gazelle Creek

Madison

3

2

To
Idaho
Falls

87

287

River

**Quake
Lake**

1

To
West
Yellowstone

**Hebgen
Lake**

Madison River—Upper
Hebgen Lake to Ennis Lake

Madison River
Hebgen Lake to Ennis Lake

Upon exiting the park, the Madison River enters the 13-mile Hebgen Lake which offers anglers a shot at the infamous gulpers—large cruising trout that readily feed on dry flies with a gluttonous, audible gulp. The Madison then thunders out of Hebgen Lake in a two-mile dash before it flows into Quake Lake. As its name implies, Quake Lake was formed during a 7.5 magnitude earthquake in 1959. A mountain collapsed dropping 80 million tons of rubble on the Madison River and adjacent campground, tragically killing 26 people.

The river gains volume from an assortment of tributaries and loses elevation quickly throughout the rapid stretch from Quake Lake to the town of Ennis (pronounced Inn-is). This world-class section of water has been accurately dubbed "The 50 Mile Riffle." Public access is excellent along Highway 287, and the wading angler will find a multitude of fishing opportunities just a short walk from the car. Float fishermen can drift this section from a boat between Lyon's Bridge and Ennis. Due to the swift water and plentiful rocks, this section should only be floated by experienced oarsmen. Wolf Creek Bridge (between Lyon's Bridge and Palisades) can be hazardous and impassible during high water.

As the Madison approaches Ennis, it braids and channels amongst thick stands of cottonwoods, forming shallow riffles and deep drop pools as the strong currents twist and turn into the Ennis reservoir. In the final seven miles of the river above the reservoir, wade fishing alone is allowed, although float fisherman can use their boat for transportation. Although this stretch is not considered technical, in late summer oarsmen can expect

Types of Fish:
Brown and Rainbow Trout, Whitefish.

Known Hatches:
Year-round: Midges. Mid March-Late April: Baetis. Late April-Mid May: Caddis. Early June-Mid July: Salmonflies, Golden Stones, Caddis. Late June-August: PMDs, Yellow Sally, Golden Stone, Hoppers, Ants, Beetles. September-Mid October: Baetis, October Caddis.

Equipment to Use:
Rods: 5-6 weight, 9 feet in length.
Lines: Floating line for dries & nymphs.
Leaders: 7½' 2-3x for nymphs, 9' 4-6x for dries, 7' 0-2x for streamers.
Wading: Difficult wading due to fast-moving riffles and slippery rocks. Felt soles are a must, and the cool water begs for waders and a wading belt during all but the hottest summer months.

Flies to Use:
Dries: Parachute Adams #12-22, BWO #18-22, Goddard's Caddis #14-18, Elk Hair Caddis #14-18, Black Caddis #16-20, Speckled X #8-10, Turk's Tarantula #8-12, Stimulator #8-16, Royal Wulff #10-16, Royal Trude #12-16, Rusty Spinner #16-18, Griffith's Gnat #18-24, PMX #8-12, Parachute Hopper #6-10, Dave's Hopper #4-10, Chernobyl Ant/Hopper #4-8, Gumby Hopper #6-10.
Nymphs: Serendipity #14-20, Hare's Ear #12-20, Sparkle Pupa #18-20, Copper John #12-18, Green & Brown Bugger #4-6, Prince Nymph #12-16, Pheasant Tail #16-20, Lightning Bug #14-18, Red San Juan Worm #6-8, Bitch Creek #2-8, Kaufmann's Gold Stone #6-10.
Streamers: Green or Brown Bugger #2-6, White, Natural or Green Zonker #2-6, Bow River Bugger #2-6, Muddler or Clouser Minnow #2-8.

Hook-up on the "50-Mile Riffle".
Photo by Brian Grossenbacher.

Floating at the base of Sphinx Mountain between McAtee and Varney Bridges.
Photo by Brian Grossenbacher.

to spend a fair bit of time scraping over rocks.

The fish in the Upper Madison benefit from nutrient-rich water, and the additional shot of aquatic life generated by the Hebgen and Earthquake lakes respectively. Anglers can find dry fly action on the Madison virtually any time of the year, including generous midge activity in the coldest months of winter. Nymph fishing is productive throughout the year with a two-fly tandem. Some of the biggest fish on the Upper Madison are caught dead drifting sculpin patterns with a small baetis nymph trailing on light tippet. This combination should be fished with plenty of weight to get the flies down in the swift currents. Any angler who has not fished the Madison should put it on their life list. Any angler who has fished the Madison cannot wait to get back.

Fishing down the middle of the upper Madison frequently produces large trout. Photo by Brian Grossenbacher.

When to Fish:

It's hard to beat a day of hopper fishing from a driftboat in July and August. Early spring offers great wade fishing opportunities without the crowds (but with unpredictable weather) or try late October for a great shot at big browns.

Seasons & Limits:

The standard fishing regulations for the *Central* and *National Park Service* fishing districts apply. Please check the *Montana Fishing Regulations and Etiquette* section.

Exceptions to Standard Regulations

Quake Lake Outlet to Lyons Bridge
Open third Saturday in May through the end of February. Catch-and-release for trout, except anglers 14 years of age and younger may take 1 trout daily and in possession, any size. Artificial lures only. Closed to fishing from boats.

Lyons Bridge to McAtee Bridge
Open third Saturday in May through the end of February. Catch-and-release for trout, except anglers 14 years of age and younger may take 1 trout daily and in possession, any size. Artifical lures only.

McAtee Bridge to Varney Bridge
Open entire year. Catch-and-release for trout, except anglers 14 years of age and younger may take 1 trout daily and in possession, any size. Artifical lures only.

Varney Bridge to Ennis Bridge
Catch-and-release for rainbow trout, except anglers 14 years of age and younger may take 1 rainbow trout daily and in possession, any size. Open entire year.

Ennis Bridge to Ennis Lake
Open third Saturday in May through the end of February. Closed to fishing from boats, although boats can be used for transportation. Catch-and-release for rainbow trout, except anglers 14 years of age and younger may take 1 rainbow trout daily and in possession, any size.

Nearby Fly Fishing:

Yellowstone National Park, Gallatin, Lower Madison, Ruby, Hebgen Lake, Cliff & Wade Lake.

Accommodations & Services:

If your fishing is focused solely upon the upper Madison, then consider staying in or around Ennis. The El Western Hotel is right on the edge of town (800-831-2773: www.elwestern.com). The Old Kirby Place, between Ennis and West Yellowstone, is a 120-year-old classic right on the Madison (888-875-8027: www.oldkirbyplace.com). For a truly Montana experience, try the Firehole Ranch outside of West Yellowstone (406-646-7294: www.fireholeranch.com). If you are combining the Madison with a trip to the Yellowstone River, Bozeman is your best bet (see the Lower Madison or Gallatin sidebars for suggestions). For campers, there are numerous options at practically every boat ramp along the river.

Rating: 9.5

This stretch of the Madison is famous the world over, which is part of the problem. I can't recall the last time I was on this stretch without at least half-a-dozen other boats, if not two dozen. With that said, it is still an excellent fishery with epic browns and rainbows, stunning vistas, numerous access points, and classic trout water. Don't forget, if you want your best shot at the big fish in this river, fish in the middle of the river (no matter how good the banks look!), and get your fly down.

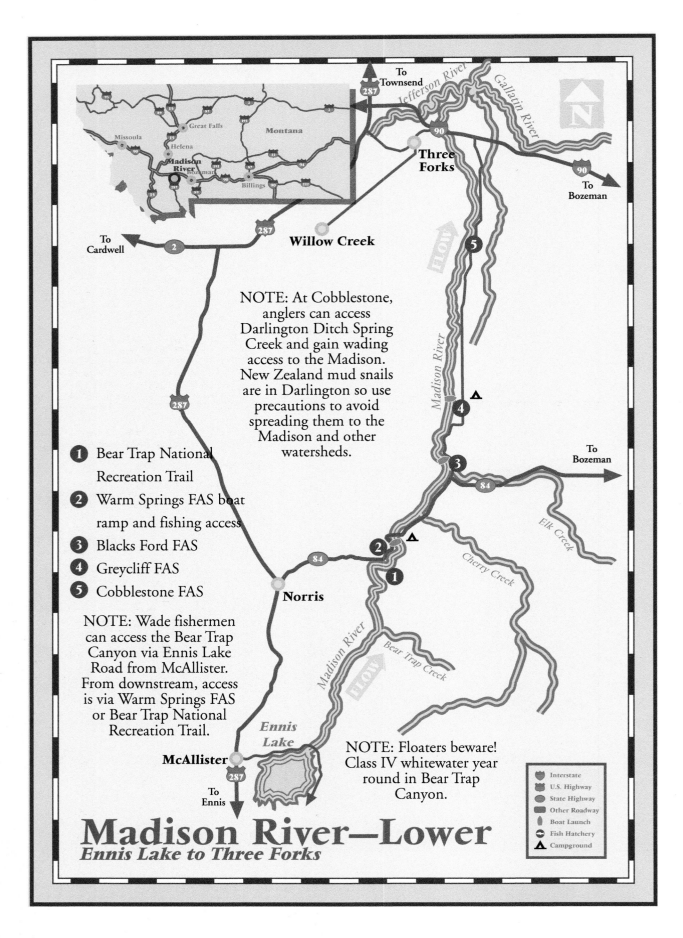

To Townsend

To Cardwell

Three Forks

To Bozeman

Willow Creek

To Bozeman

NOTE: At Cobblestone, anglers can access Darlington Ditch Spring Creek and gain wading access to the Madison. New Zealand mud snails are in Darlington so use precautions to avoid spreading them to the Madison and other watersheds.

① Bear Trap National Recreation Trail

② Warm Springs FAS boat ramp and fishing access

③ Blacks Ford FAS

④ Greycliff FAS

⑤ Cobblestone FAS

NOTE: Wade fishermen can access the Bear Trap Canyon via Ennis Lake Road from McAllister. From downstream, access is via Warm Springs FAS or Bear Trap National Recreation Trail.

Norris

Ennis Lake

McAllister

To Ennis

NOTE: Floaters beware! Class IV whitewater year round in Bear Trap Canyon.

Madison River

Jefferson River

Gallatin River

Madison River

Elk Creek

Cherry Creek

Bear Trap Creek

Madison River

FLOW

FLOW

Interstate
U.S. Highway
State Highway
Other Roadway
Boat Launch
Fish Hatchery
Campground

Madison River—Lower
Ennis Lake to Three Forks

Madison River
Ennis Lake to Three Forks

Exiting the shallow Ennis Reservoir, the Madison pours into the Bear Trap canyon with enough energy to earn its Class IV whitewater status year-round. Hiking trails parallel the river throughout this 7-mile canyon. Access is available at the dam or via the Warm Springs fishing access at the bottom of the canyon where Highway 84 joins the river. Keep your eyes to the ground throughout this region as rattlesnakes are prevalent.

The Lower Madison is best fished during the spring, early summer and the fall as the shallow water in the Ennis Reservoir superheats during the hot summer months, and the fish downstream take shelter in the cooler tributaries. The Lower Madison is easily wadeable with a sandy, weedy bottom. A prolific population of crayfish provides a "Miracle Grow" effect on these broad shouldered trout. Fish and aquatic insects alike proliferate in the shelter of the numerous weed beds that make up the river bottom. Upon cursory examination, the Madison appears to be one large channel without any character. Closer inspection reveals subtle pockets and seams as the water passes over and around the weed beds. Fish in the Lower Madison literally have productive holding water from bank to bank the entire 18 miles from the dam to Three Forks. Although the numbers of trout decrease as the river approaches Three Forks, average size increases and fishing pressure decreases, providing an angler with an opportunity for a true trophy trout.

The Lower Madison really shines from March through early July as hatches seem to overlap each other, providing excellent

Types of Fish:
Brown and Rainbow Trout, Whitefish.

Known Hatches:
Year-round: Midges.
Mid March-Late April: Baetis.
Late April-July: Caddis.
June: Salmonflies.
Early June-Mid July: Golden Stones.
September-Mid October: Baetis, Crawdads/Crayfish, October Caddis.

Equipment to Use:
Rods: 5-6 weight, 9 feet in length.
Lines: Floating line for dries & nymphs.
Leaders: 9' 3-6x for dries, 7½' 2-4x for nymphs, 7' 0-2x for streamers.
Wading: Shallow, easily-wadable river. Wet-wade early summer and fall, otherwise full waders and wading belt.

Flies to Use:
Dries: Parachute Adams #16-22, BWO #18-20, Goddard's Caddis #14-18, Elk Hair Caddis #14-18, PMX #8-12, Speckled X #8-10.
Nymphs: Hare's Ear #16-20, Sparkle Pupa #14-18, Copper John #12-18, Green & Brown Bugger #4-6, Prince Nymph #12-16, Pheasant Tail #16-20, Lightning Bug #14-18, Serendipity #14-18, Red San Juan Worm #6-8, Clouser Crayfish #2-8.
Streamers: Green or Brown Bugger #2-6, White, Natural or Green Zonker #2-6, Bow River Bugger #2-6.

When to Fish:
The lower Madison is an amazing river for large browns and healthy rainbows as long as you aren't there in the heat of summer. Ennis Reservoir warms up the lower stretch of the river below the dam and, with the exception of the Bear Trap Wilderness area, we typically do not fish the lower Madison from mid-July through August. Warmer water and proximity to Bozeman also

Angler enjoying a quiet evening on the lower Madison.
Photo by Brian Grossenbacher.

The water from Black's Ford to Three Forks holds some of the largest fish in the Madison.
Photo by Brian Grossenbacher.

dry fly fishing. The cool nights of September re-energize the fish and some real monsters appear as the browns begin to spawn. Although the Lower Madison is a wonderful dry fly fishery, it typically reserves the best fish for nymph and streamer fishermen. A productive combination is to dead drift a crayfish pattern or sculpin with a small nymph (#16-#18 dropper). Twenty-plus-inch fish are not uncommon in this section, so make sure your knots are strong, and you have plenty of backing on your reel.

The weedy, shallow nature of this river can sometimes leave the veteran fisherman trying to decipher between a light take and a bottom hit. On the other hand, eager, beginner fishermen often do surprisingly well due to their willingness to set the hook on every bump of the strike indicator. For spring and fall this river arguably can't be beat within a hundred square miles. Keep your eyes to the ground for rattlesnakes and poison ivy.

Craig Boyd and John Waller with a nice Madison River brown.
Photo by Brian Grossenbacher.

brings an armada of recreational floaters. If you don't mind cold weather and snow, fishing in March, April and early May can be truly fantastic. If you miss the epic Mother's Day caddis hatch you'll still have plenty of baetis around to keep you and the fish satisfied. In the fall, the return of the baetis and the molting crayfish drive the trout mad.

Seasons & Limits:
The standard fishing regulations for the *Central* fishing district apply. Please check the *Montana Fishing Regulations and Etiquette* section.
Exceptions to Standard Regulations
Ennis Dam to the mouth
  Open entire year.

Nearby Fly Fishing:
Yellowstone National Park, Gallatin, Yellowstone, Paradise Valley Spring Creeks, Upper Madison, Ruby, Missouri.

Accommodations & Services:
Bozeman is a 20+ minute drive away and offers numerous lodging options. Below are a few of our favorites: The Gallatin Gateway Inn (800-676-3522: www.gallatingatewayinn.com) was built in 1927 as a stopping point for the Chicago/Milwaukee railroad. This historically-restored inn located south of Bozeman, offers a five-star restaurant, cigar-friendly bar, incomparable atmosphere and comfortable rooms.
For a vacation home, try Mountain Home Vacation Rentals (800-550-4589: www.mountain-home.com). If you are into wolves, B&Bs, and are planning to fish both the Madison and Yellowstone, check out Howler's Inn (406-586-0304: www.howlersinn.com). There are several camping sites along the river, but if it's a weekend get there early. Greycliff Campground is a few miles North of Black's Ford boat access. There are also several campsites north and south of the bridge.

Bozeman has the best restaurant selection around. One favorite is Montana Ale Works, downtown on Main Street. They offer a full bar, countless beers on tap, and a great and varied menu. An unexpected find on Main Street is Plunk, a wonderfully quaint, yet hip wine bar with an excellent chef. A client favorite for higher end dining is Boodles on Main Street with live jazz on the weekends and a great chef. Need a great martini, cigar and a trout appetizer? Try the Mint on Main Street in Belgrade. BBQ? Tromp on over to Bar 3 BBQ, also in Belgrade. Pizza? Try MacKenzie River Pizza downtown on Main Street. If you aren't in a hurry, go sit on the patio of The Garage and sip a cold one while waiting on a great burger, grilled salmon or salad.

Coffee shops are on just about every block. The Community Co-Op on Main Street offers organic coffees and teas and wireless Internet. Rocky Mountain Roasting Company offers several locations around town with great coffee and free wireless. For a tasty and filling breakfast or lunch try the Community Co-Op, Main Street Over Easy, the Cat Eye or the epic breakfast burrito at Soby's in the old Bozeman Hotel.

Rating: 8.5
If you are fishing the lower Madison in April, May, June, early-July, September or October, then we'd have to say 9+. August, just don't do it. The lower Madison offers an excellent opportunity to catch multiple 18"+ fat, healthy, brown trout and hefty rainbows as well.

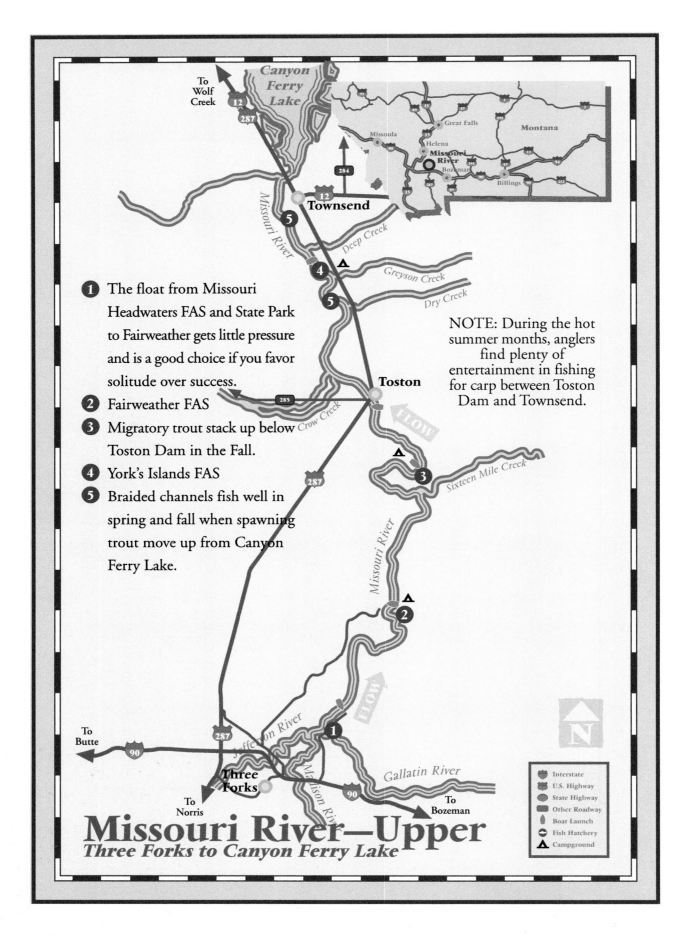

To Wolf Creek

Canyon Ferry Lake

12
287

284

Townsend

Missouri River

Deep Creek

Greyson Creek

Dry Creek

1 The float from Missouri Headwaters FAS and State Park to Fairweather gets little pressure and is a good choice if you favor solitude over success.

2 Fairweather FAS

3 Migratory trout stack up below Toston Dam in the Fall.

4 York's Islands FAS

5 Braided channels fish well in spring and fall when spawning trout move up from Canyon Ferry Lake.

Toston

285

Crow Creek

NOTE: During the hot summer months, anglers find plenty of entertainment in fishing for carp between Toston Dam and Townsend.

FLOW

Sixteen Mile Creek

287

Missouri River

FLOW

To Butte

90

287

Jefferson River

Three Forks

Madison River

90

Gallatin River

To Norris

To Bozeman

N

Interstate
U.S. Highway
State Highway
Other Roadway
Boat Launch
Fish Hatchery
Campground

Montana map inset:
Missoula, Great Falls, Helena, Missouri River, Bozeman, Billings

Missouri River—Upper
Three Forks to Canyon Ferry Lake

Missouri River

Three Forks to Canyon Ferry Lake

The Missouri river has changed dramatically since Lewis and Clark led their expedition to its headwaters just over 200 years ago. Most notably, the river's flow is interrupted by dams at four locations in its upper reaches for the purposes of irrigation and power. That is not to say that the dams are all bad—especially for those in search of trout. The dams allow for sediment and warmer water from irrigation returns to settle and cool in the depths of reservoirs, especially Canyon Ferry, Hauser and Holter. In fact, the Missouri river owes its healthy trout population and its spring creek qualities to the cooling and filtering that take place in the reservoirs along its length.

The Missouri runs shallow, wide, warm and leisurely from its headwaters just outside of Three Forks. With temperatures climbing in the summer months, the best fishing is found in the spring and fall. This section is best fished subsurface with streamers and large nymphs.

From the Toston dam to Canyon Ferry Lake, the river gains a bit in speed but still suffers from warm temperatures. Again, spring and fall represent the best time for trout—especially the lunkers that make their way from Canyon Ferry Lake to spawn in the braided channels upstream from the mouth of the lake.

Types of Fish:
Brown and Rainbow Trout, Carp, Walleye, Northern Pike, Small-Mouth Bass, Whitefish.

Known Hatches:
Year-round: Midges, Streamers.
Mid March-Late April: Baetis.
Late April-Mid July: Caddis.
Late June-July: PMDs, Caddis, Hoppers, Ants, Beetles.
September-Mid October: Tricos, Baetis, Streamers.

Equipment to Use:
Rods: 5-7 weight, 8-9 feet in length.
Lines: Floating line for dries & nymphs, sink tip line for streamers.
Leaders: 9' 4-5x for nymphs, 12' 5-7x for dries, 7' 0-2x for streamers.
Wading: Best fished by a drift boat due to the size of the river. However, slow flows allow for easy wading throughout most of the river. Chest-high waders recommended.

Flies to Use:
Dries: Parachute Adams #16-22, BWO #18-22, Goddard's Caddis #14-18, Elk Hair Caddis #14-18, Trico #18-22, Royal Wulff #12-16, Griffith's Gnat #18-24, PMX #8-12, Parachute Hopper #6-10, Gumby Hopper #6-10, Turk's Tarantula #6-10, Red or Black Flying Ant #16-20.
Nymphs: Hare's Ear #12-20, Copper Johns #12-18, Sparkle Pupa #18-20, Midge Pupa #18-22, Prince Nymph #12-18, Pheasant Tail #12-20, Lightning Bug #12-18, Serendipity #14-18, Red San Juan Worm #6-8, Scud #16-20, Green & Brown Bugger #2-6, Crayfish #2-8.
(Continued)

Wet wading is a great way to stay cool.
Photo by Brian Grossenbacher.

Winter dry fly fishing on the Missouri.
Photo by Brian Grossenbacher.

For the angler who seeks a bent rod and doesn't care what bends it, the summer months on this stretch offer ample opportunities to fish for carp. Don't turn your nose up too fast on these wily fish ranging from 5 to 15+ pounds. Carp will eagerly take a dry. Tricos and hoppers seem to be their preferred top-water fare, and they will inhale a small streamer or crayfish pattern sub-surface, if presented within their narrow feeding window.

Flies to Use: (Continued)

Streamers: Green, Brown, Black or Light-Olive Bugger #2-6, Clouser or Muddler Minnow #2-6, JJ Special #2-8, Sculpin #2-8, Leeches #2-8, Green, White or Natural Zonkers #2-6.

When to Fish:

Typically avoid the late summer.

Seasons & Limits:

The standard fishing regulations for the *Central* and *Eastern* fishing districts apply. Please check the *Montana Fishing Regulations and Etiquette* section.

Exceptions to Standard Regulations

Entire River

    Open entire year.

    Catch-and-release for cutthroat trout.

Toston Dam to Canyon Ferry Reservoir

    Localized spawning areas closed as posted from March 1 through June 15.

    Combined Trout: catch-and-release for brown trout between 18 and 24 inches.

    Walleye: 20 daily and 40 in possession.

Nearby Fly Fishing:

Madison, Canyon Ferry Reservoir, Gallatin, Jefferson.

Accommodations & Services:

In Three Forks your best bet for lodging is the enchanting Sacajawea Hotel (406-285-6515: www.sacajaweahotel.com). There is a vast assortment of options in the capital city of Helena (Wingate Inn, 406-449-3000, Hampton Inn, 406-443-5800).

Rating: 7

The upper section of the Missouri is not the one of fabled lore, however numerous fishing opportunities do exist, including the engaging art of catching carp on a dry fly.

Missouri River carp will readily rise to a well-presented dry fly, in this case to Tom Fournie's hopper. Photo by Brian Grossenbacher.

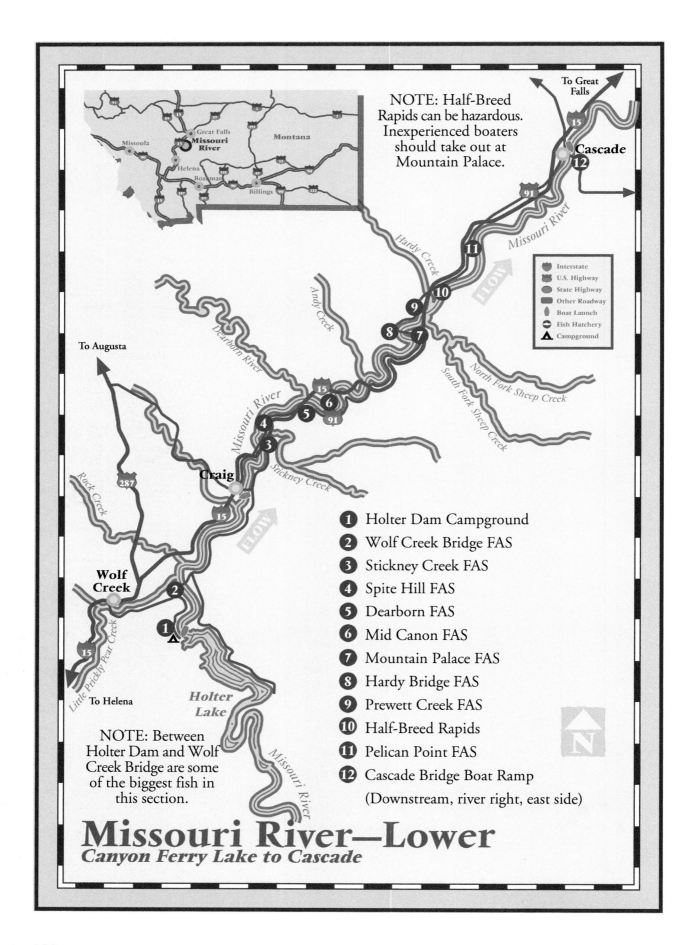

NOTE: Half-Breed Rapids can be hazardous. Inexperienced boaters should take out at Mountain Palace.

To Great Falls

Cascade

Missouri River

Hardy Creek

Andy Creek

North Fork Sheep Creek

South Fork Sheep Creek

Dearborn River

Missouri River

To Augusta

Stickney Creek

Craig

Rock Creek

Wolf Creek

Little Prickly Pear Creek

To Helena

Holter Lake

Missouri River

Interstate
U.S. Highway
State Highway
Other Roadway
Boat Launch
Fish Hatchery
Campground

1 Holter Dam Campground
2 Wolf Creek Bridge FAS
3 Stickney Creek FAS
4 Spite Hill FAS
5 Dearborn FAS
6 Mid Canon FAS
7 Mountain Palace FAS
8 Hardy Bridge FAS
9 Prewett Creek FAS
10 Half-Breed Rapids
11 Pelican Point FAS
12 Cascade Bridge Boat Ramp
(Downstream, river right, east side)

NOTE: Between Holter Dam and Wolf Creek Bridge are some of the biggest fish in this section.

N

Missouri River—Lower
Canyon Ferry Lake to Cascade

Missouri River
Canyon Ferry Lake
to Cascade

The Missouri River from Canyon Ferry dam to Hauser Lake although short, enjoys productive and popular spawning runs in the spring and fall for rainbows and browns. Be prepared to share this busy stretch with fellow anglers also in search of trophy trout. Scuds, San Juan Worms, and bright egg patterns are the most productive patterns. Please wade carefully to avoid spawning redds. Always land fish as quickly as possible, and handle them carefully to promote the health of future trout classes.

The water between Hauser and Holter lakes is similar to the previous stretch in that large fish move out of Holter Lake to spawn. Accordingly, it fishes best spring and fall, and particularly well in the spring when the rainbows spawn. Access can be difficult and this stretch receives a tremendous amount of pressure from spin, fly and bait fishermen. If you are looking for a peaceful flyfishing experience, this is definitely not the place for you. If you are looking to hook a fish of a lifetime, and you don't mind crowds, then get on the water early and mark your spot. Access to the dam fluctuates with current security alerts, so check with local fly shops before you head out. Or, you can access the river at the confluence of Beaver Creek via Beaver

Types of Fish:
Brown and Rainbow Trout, Carp, Walleye, Northern Pike, Small-Mouth Bass, Whitefish.

Known Hatches:
Year-round: Midges.
Mid March-Late April: Baetis.
Late April-Mid July: Caddis.
Late June-July: PMDs, Caddis, Ants, Beetles, Tricos.
Late August-Mid October: Hoppers, Tricos, Baetis, Streamers.

Equipment to Use:
Rods: 5-7 weight, 8½-9 feet in length.
Lines: Floating line for dries & nymphs, sink tip line for streamers.
Leaders: 9' 4-5x for nymphs, 12' 5-7x for dries, 7' 0-2x for streamers.
Wading: Best fished by a drift boat, due to the size of the river. However, slow flows and a flat bottom allow for easy wading throughout most of the river. Chest-high waders recommended.

Flies to Use:
Dries: Parachute Adams #16-22, BWO #18-24, Goddard's Caddis #14-18, Elk Hair Caddis #14-18, Trico #18-22, Royal Wulff #12-16, Rusty Spinner #16-18, Griffith's Gnat #18-24, PMX #8-12, Parachute Hopper #6-10, Gumby Hopper #6-10, Turk's Tarantula #6-10, Red or Black Flying Ant #16-20.
Nymphs: Hare's Ear #16-20, Sparkle Pupa #18-20, Midge Pupa #18-22, Prince Nymph #14-18, Pheasant Tail #16-22, Lightning Bug #16-20, Serendipity #14-18, Red San Juan Worm #6-8, Pink Scud #16-20, Green & Brown Bugger #2-6.
Streamers: Green, Brown, Black or Light-Olive Bugger #2-6, Clouser or Muddler Minnow #2-6, JJ Special #2-8, Sculpin #2-8, Leeches #2-8, Green, White or Natural Zonkers #2-6.

Evening float above Craig, Montana. Photo by Brian Grossenbacher.

The Missouri fishes well from bank to bank with fish often congregating on current seams, back eddies, and structure.
Photo by Brian Grossenbacher.

Creek Road, a 4WD road from the town of York. The water between Beaver Creek and the dam affords great sight fishing opportunities to groups of large fish.

The 48 miles of river between Holter dam and Cascade offer the angler the best year-round fishing opportunities on the Missouri river. Access is good and the smooth bottom provides firm footing for the wading angler. That being said, the Missouri is approximately 100-yards wide in this section so a drift boat is an excellent way to cover this large body of water. Floaters find this stretch easy to navigate, with the only exception being Half Breed Rapids below Sheep Creek. Inexperienced boaters should take out at Mountain Palace. This stretch fishes very much like a spring creek, and the fish hold in pods. Once on a pod of rising fish, you may find yourself there for hours. Prolific hatches of baetis, caddis, tricos, Pale Morning Duns and terrestrials such as hoppers, beetles, and ants will keep the dry fly fisherman entertained from early April through late October. Nymph fishermen will do best with long leaders, fluorocarbon tippet and a two-fly rig. Fish a larger nymph such as a girdle bug first, and drop a smaller fly such as a pheasant tail or scud off the bend of the hook with 16"-18" of tippet. Do not be afraid to use plenty of weight to get your flies down in the deeper runs. Although you may find the greatest numbers of fish in deeper water, the largest fish in this section prefer the shallower riffles and bank structure. Keep moving, and explore the Missouri from bank to bank.

A large spring brown in hand.
Photo by Brian Grossenbacher.

When to Fish:
Excellent dry fly fishing can be had practically year-round on the Missouri. Spring and Fall are especially good times to fish. Late summer should typically be avoided.

Seasons & Limits:
The standard fishing regulations for the *Central* and *Eastern* fishing districts apply. Please check the *Montana Fishing Regulations and Etiquette* section.
Exceptions to Standard Regulations
Entire River
    Open entire year. Catch-and-release for cutthroat trout.
Toston Dam to Canyon Ferry Reservoir
    Localized spawning areas closed as posted from March 1 through June 15. Combined Trout: catch-and-release for brown trout between 18 and 24 inches. Walleye: 20 daily and 40 in possession.
Canyon Ferry Reservoir
    See Canyon Ferry Reservoir regulations.
Downstream from Canyon Ferry Dam to Hauser Reservoir
    See Hauser Reservoir regulations.
Hauser Dam to American Bar Gulch (Approx. 4.6 miles downstream from Hauser Dam)
    Catch-and-release for brown trout. Walleye: 6 daily and in possession, includes 5 under 20 inches and 1 over 28 inches.
Downstream from American Bar Gulch to Holter Reservoir
    See Holter Reservoir regulations.
Holter Dam to mouth of Dearborn River
    Combined Trout: 1 rainbow trout (any size) daily and in possession and 1 brown trout (22-inch minimum) daily and in possession.
Craig Bridge to Sheep Creek Bridge
    Spearing: open for up to 5 whitefish daily with rubber or spring-propelled spears by persons swimming or submerged.
Mouth of Dearborn River to Cascade Bridge
    Combined Trout: 3 rainbow trout daily and in possession, only 1 over 16 inches and 1 brown trout daily and in possession, 22-inch minimum.

Nearby Fly Fishing:
Madison, Blackfoot, Canyon Ferry Reservoir, Jefferson.

Accommodations & Services:
The 'one-stop' place to go for food, lodging, flies, shuttles and excellent advice is The Trout Shop in Craig (800-337-8528: www.thetroutshop.com).

Rating: 9.5
Although several years of drought have reduced the average number of trout, there are still more than 3,000 rainbow trout and 600+ brown trout per mile, many of which tape out over 18". Even with the reduction in numbers, biologists and locals alike have pointed out that the fish are healthier than in past years. The Missouri is still a fantastic option for catching trophy trout. Crowding can be an issue, in spring and fall, yet this is one river not to be missed by the consummate fly fisherman.

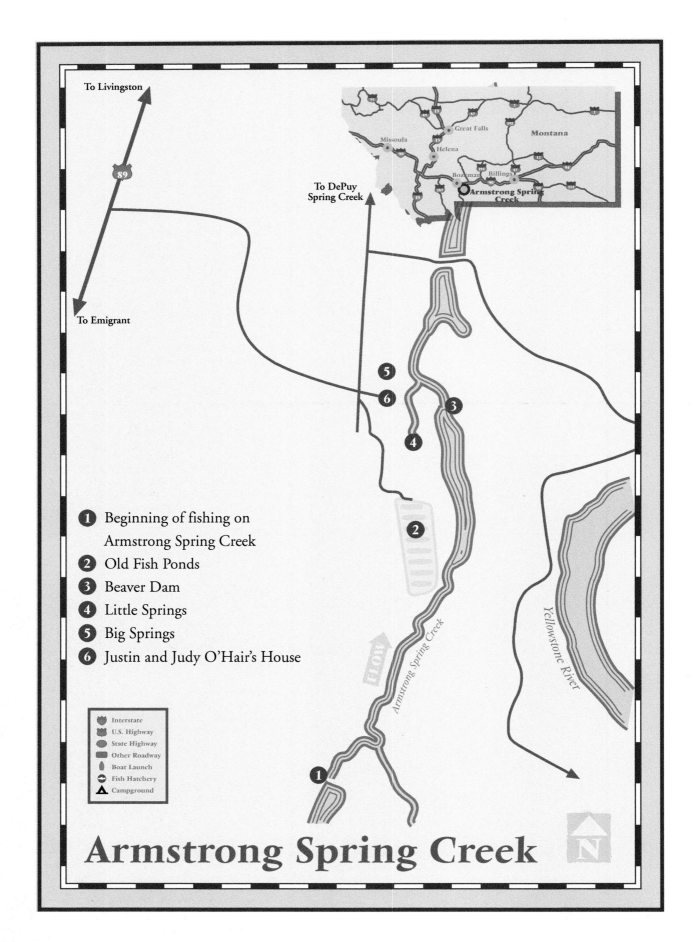

To Livingston

89

To Emigrant

To DePuy
Spring Creek

Montana

Great Falls

Missoula

Helena

Bozeman   Billings

Armstrong Spring Creek

5

6

3

4

1 Beginning of fishing on
Armstrong Spring Creek
2 Old Fish Ponds
3 Beaver Dam
4 Little Springs
5 Big Springs
6 Justin and Judy O'Hair's House

2

FLOW

Armstrong Spring Creek

Yellowstone River

1

Interstate
U.S. Highway
State Highway
Other Roadway
Boat Launch
Fish Hatchery
Campground

Armstrong Spring Creek

N

Paradise Valley Spring Creeks

The Paradise Valley is home to three of the most prolific spring creek fisheries found in the western United States, Armstrong's, DePuy's, and Nelson's. Nestled in a setting that blurs the line between pastoral and picturesque, these creeks offer phenomenal, yet technical fishing. As the creeks twist through stands of mature cottonwoods and lush pastureland, the Absaroka Mountain Range looms conspicuously in the background with a compelling beauty that steals attention even in the midst of heavily rising fish.

The nutrient-rich waters of these creeks are home to a strong resident population of trout, but perhaps more importantly, they serve as invaluable spawning habitat for Yellowstone River rainbow, cutthroat and brown trout. The water consistently flows from the ground at 53 degrees providing ideal fishing conditions year-round. The character of the water varies from long, slow, gin-clear pools, to cascading riffles and deep holding pockets. The stream bottoms range from cobbled rocks and fine gravel, to sand, with generous weed growth throughout. The heavy weed growth provides excellent habitat for the varied and hearty aquatic insect population.

Of the three creeks, Armstrong's seems to have the greatest concentration of fish throughout the year, and the headwaters of Armstrong's literally bubbles from the ground in the middle of a pasture. The stream varies from 30' to 80' wide and features classic riffle run pool characteristics. Armstrong's allows 12 anglers per day, which seems crowded when the creek is fully booked.

Types of Fish:
Yellowstone Cutthroat, Brown, and Rainbow Trout, Whitefish.

Known Hatches:
Year-round: Midges.
Mid March-Late April: Baetis.
Late April-August: Caddis.
Early June-mid July: Salmonflies, Golden Stones.
July-August: PMDs, Yellow Sallies, Hoppers, Tricos, Green Drake, Sulphurs.
September-Mid October: Baetis.

Equipment to Use:
Rods: 4-5 weight, 8-9 feet in length.
Lines: Floating line for dries & nymphs, sink tip for streamers in pond at Depuy's.
Leaders: 10-12' 5-7x for dries, 9' 4-5x for nymphs, 7' 0-2x for streamers.
Wading: Easy wading, but water temperatures are cool (42-60 degrees). Waders are typically warranted, except in late summer.

Flies to Use:
Dries: Cluster Midge #18-24, Griffith's Gnat #18-24, Parachute Adams #16-24, BWO #18-22, CDC Baetis #18-22, RS-2 #18-22, Goddard's Caddis #14-18, Elk Hair Caddis #14-18, Black Caddis #18-22, Rusty Spinner #16-20, Sparkle Dun #16-20, CDC Emerger #16-20, Harrop No-Hackle #18-22, Para Hare's Ear #18-20, Sparkle Dun Callibaetis #18-20.
Nymphs: Brassie #18-24, Palomino Midge #18-24, Disco Midge #18-24, Zebra Midge #18-22, Miracle Midge #18-22, Sparkle Pupa #18-20, Sawyer Pheasant Tail #16-22, Hare's Ear #16-20, Sow Bug #14-18, Olive Sparkle Scud #14-18, San Juan Worm #12-20, Dave's Emerger #18-22, Lightning Bug #18-20.
Streamers: Green, Brown or Black Bugger #2-6, White, Natural or Green Zonker #2-6.

Winter midge fishing on the spring creeks holds dry fly aficionados over 'til spring.
Photo by Brian Grossenbacher.

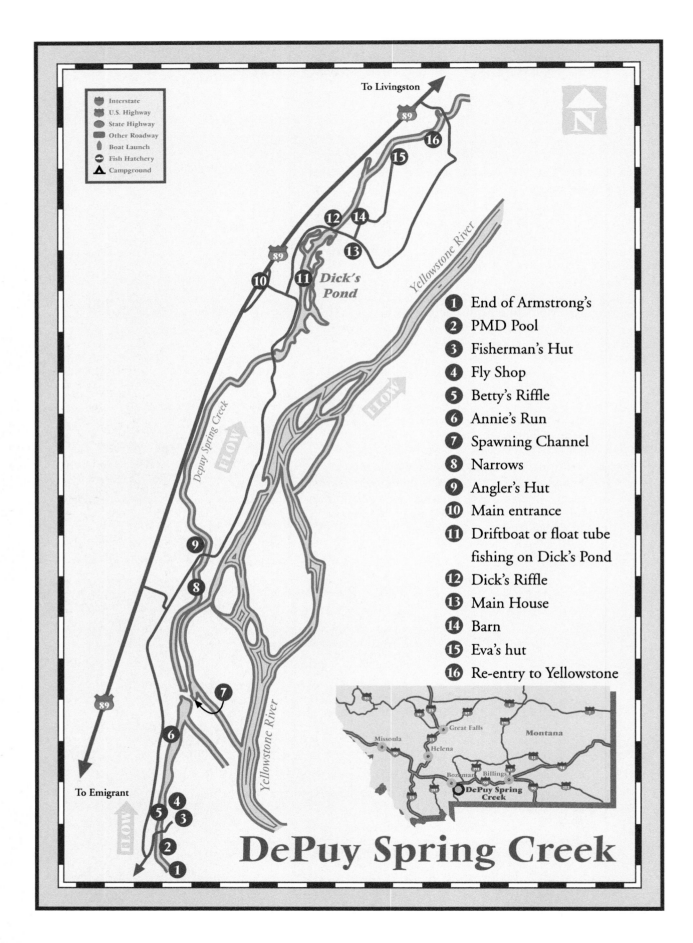

Legend
- Interstate
- U.S. Highway
- State Highway
- Other Roadway
- Boat Launch
- Fish Hatchery
- Campground

To Livingston

Yellowstone River

Dick's Pond

DePuy Spring Creek

To Emigrant

1. End of Armstrong's
2. PMD Pool
3. Fisherman's Hut
4. Fly Shop
5. Betty's Riffle
6. Annie's Run
7. Spawning Channel
8. Narrows
9. Angler's Hut
10. Main entrance
11. Driftboat or float tube fishing on Dick's Pond
12. Dick's Riffle
13. Main House
14. Barn
15. Eva's hut
16. Re-entry to Yellowstone

Montana

Great Falls
Missoula
Helena
Bozeman Billings
DePuy Spring Creek

DePuy Spring Creek

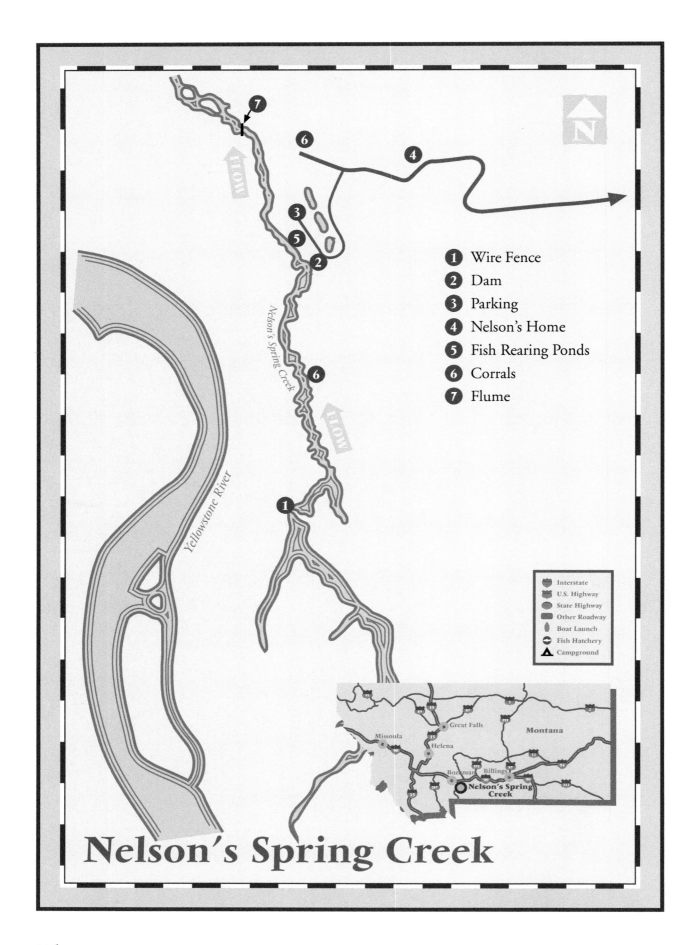

1 Wire Fence
2 Dam
3 Parking
4 Nelson's Home
5 Fish Rearing Ponds
6 Corrals
7 Flume

Interstate
U.S. Highway
State Highway
Other Roadway
Boat Launch
Fish Hatchery
Campground

Nelson's Spring Creek

Checking in at DePuy's is worth the price of admission. The late Warren DePuy built his home based on a picture in a Southern Living Calendar for which he never had a set of plans. Although this "Tara" look-alike seems out of place in Montana, its rich character and unique design speaks volumes about this independent family. Originally, Armstrong's Spring Creek ran onto the DePuy property for about a quarter mile before it dumped into the Yellowstone. When Warren DePuy decided he wanted a fishery on his property, he simply redirected the stream into an old Yellowstone stream bed with the help of a ranch tractor, and virtually overnight he had 3 miles of private spring creek. Numerous improvements have been made to the creek over the years, and today DePuy's enjoys the greatest variety and quantity of water of all three creeks. DePuy's allows 16 anglers per day.

Although the smallest of the three creeks, Nelson's has found a healthy balance by only allowing five anglers per day. Recent stream work has removed choking silt from the upper reaches of the creek, and the hatches and fish counts are healthier than ever.

Though the Paradise Valley spring creeks are a memorable experience for any level angler they are not the place for a rank beginner to jump into the sport. Instead, anglers can expect technical fishing with small flies, fine tippets, and well-schooled trout.

The rod fees on all three creeks range from $40-$100 depending upon the time of the year, and even though they often book well in advance, last minute reservations are often available.

Armstrong Spring Creek, 1 ¼ Miles: (406) 222-2979
DePuy Spring Creek, 3 Miles: (406) 222-0221
Nelson's Spring Creek, ¾ Mile: (406) 222-6560

Spring creek fishing at its best.
Photo by Brian Grossenbacher.

When to Fish:

The Spring Creeks fish well year-round due to constant water temperature, and are often the saving grace during spring runoff and winter. Any day of the year you can fish dries on the spring creeks, be it midges, baetis, caddis, PMDs, yellow Sallies, tricos or numerous other hatches.

Seasons & Limits:

Due to the fact that all of the Spring Creeks are private water (rod fee required), there are no state regulations. Because the spring creeks are home to critical spawning beds, shallow riffles and redds should be avoided during spring (rainbow spawn), early summer (cutthroat spawn) and fall (brown spawn).

Nearby Fly Fishing:

Yellowstone National Park, Yellowstone, Madison, Gallatin, Boulder.

Accommodations & Services:

Livingston and Bozeman offer countless options. Below are a few of our favorites in Livingston. See the lower Madison or Gallatin for suggestions for Bozeman.
The Yellowstone House (406-586-1922: www.yellowstonehouse.com) is a lovely riverside cabin with access to the local Chico Hot Springs. It holds 8+ adults, or the Honeymoon Cabin is great for a couple.
For B&Bs, check out Howler's Inn (406-586-0304: www.howlersinn.com). The quaint country setting halfway between Bozeman and Livingston, and the howling wolves, make for a great option.
To follow in the footsteps of Buffalo Bill and Calamity Jane, try a true cowboy hotel right in the heart of Livingston, The Murray Hotel (406-222-1350: www.murrayhotel.com) or the 100+ year old Chico Hot Springs Lodge.
Several campgrounds are along the river: Paradise, Loch Leven and Mallards Rest, as well as a great KOA right on the Yellowstone at Pine Creek. A couple hundred yards up the road is the tiny town of Pine Creek and a café that has outdoor concerts and BBQs on the weekends in the summer.
For other restaurants, don't miss the Rib & Chop House in town, and Russell Chatham's Livingston Bar & Grill. If you are farther south, and in the mood for a 5-star meal, try Chico Hot Springs Lodge (406-333-4933: www.chicohotsprings.com).

Rating: 9.5

Anglers world-wide dream of fishing the heralded Paradise Valley Spring Creeks. The sheer size and number of fish are certainly part of the reason. Add to that, stunning scenery, proximity to the Yellowstone River and Yellowstone National Park, and the thrill and reward of technical fishing, and you'll understand why the creeks are often booked months in advance.

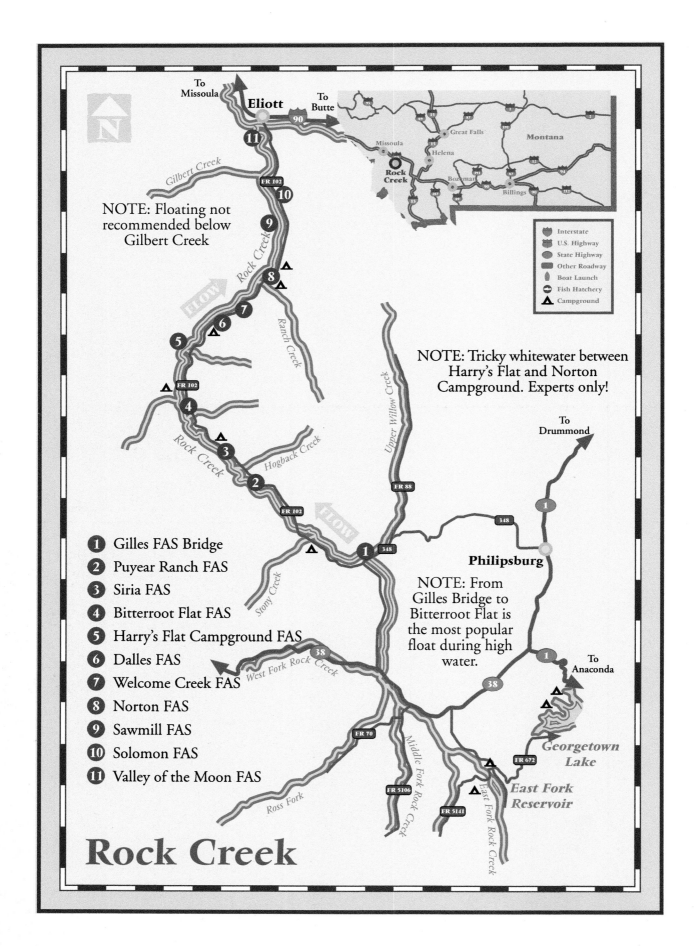

NOTE: Floating not recommended below Gilbert Creek

NOTE: Tricky whitewater between Harry's Flat and Norton Campground. Experts only!

NOTE: From Gilles Bridge to Bitterroot Flat is the most popular float during high water.

Legend
- Interstate
- U.S. Highway
- State Highway
- Other Roadway
- Boat Launch
- Fish Hatchery
- Campground

1 Gilles FAS Bridge
2 Puyear Ranch FAS
3 Siria FAS
4 Bitterroot Flat FAS
5 Harry's Flat Campground FAS
6 Dalles FAS
7 Welcome Creek FAS
8 Norton FAS
9 Sawmill FAS
10 Solomon FAS
11 Valley of the Moon FAS

Rock Creek

Rock Creek

Rock Creek is the quintessential freestone trout stream in Western Montana. Careful regulations, limited development and ready access, all contribute to the allure of Rock Creek. Yet, when you add a healthy trout population and bountiful aquatic life, the picture is complete. From its modest beginnings between the John Long and Sapphire Mountains at the confluence of its East, Middle and West forks, Rock Creek tumbles 52 miles to the Clark Fork. Rock Creek is an excellent choice for anglers of all ability levels and is the best place around Missoula to view big game including bighorn sheep, elk, deer, moose, and less frequently black bear and mountain lion. Rock Creek is a perennial favorite to anyone who has ever wet a line in its rushing waters.

Rock Creek runs through National Forest land for much of its course and is paralleled by Rock Creek Road creating easy access for the wading angler. The river above Gilles Bridge is a slower moving meadow stream with 10"-12" westslope cutthroat and the occasional brookie. Most anglers concentrate on the section downstream from Gilles Bridge as the volume of water and size of the fish increases substantially. Rainbow trout become more prevalent as you continue downstream and the average size jumps up to 14". From Harry's Flat Campground to the confluence with the Clark Fork, the river becomes more of a brown trout fishery with riffle, run and pool characteristics. As a general rule, this is where the larger fish in Rock Creek are caught, partially due to a population of migratory browns that move in from the Clark Fork to spawn in the fall.

Types of Fish:
Brook, Brown, Bull, Westslope Cutthroat and Rainbow Trout, Whitefish.

Known Hatches:
March-April: Baetis, March Browns, Skwalas.
April-May: Green Drakes, Mahogany Duns, Baetis.
May-June: Caddis, Skwalas, Green Drakes.
June-July: Salmonflies, Golden Stones, Yellow Sallies, PMDs.
August-September: Tricos, craneflies, hoppers, PMDs.

Equipment to Use:
Rods: 4-5 weight, 8-9 feet in length.
Lines: Floating line for dries and nymphs.
Leaders: 7½'-9' 3-4x for nymphs, 9'-10' 4-5x for dries, 7' 0-2X for streamers.

Flies to Use:
Dries: Parachute Adams #12-20, CDC Green Drake #10-16, Parachute Stone #10-12, Stimulator #4-16, Skwala Stonefly Dry #10-12, Elk Hair Caddis #10-16, Foam Yellow Sally #12-18, Sparkle Dun #16-18, Rusty Spinner #16, PMX #10-14, Turk's Tarantula #8-10, Royal Wulff #10-16, Ants & Beetles #12-20.
Nymphs: Olive Hare's Ear #10-14, Brook's Stone #2-8, Black & Orange Rubber Legs #2-8, Poxyback Stone Nymph #6-16, Kaufman's Gold Stone #2-12, Bitch Creek #2-8, Brown Stone Rubber Leg #8-10, Trico Nymph #18-22, Copper John #10-16, Prince Nymph #10-16, Lightning Bug #12-18, San Juan Worm.
Streamers: Woolly Buggers #4-8, Muddler and Clouser Minnow #4-8, JJ Special #4-8, Shenk's Scuplin #4-8.

Rock Creek's course through National Forest land creates excellent access for wading anglers. Photo by Brian Grossenbacher.

Anglers enjoy the fall baetis hatch on Rock Creek.
Photo by Brian Grossenbacher.

Rock Creek is best known for its prolific salmonfly hatch that kicks off between late May and early June. The word is out on this hatch so expect to share the water with plenty of fellow anglers. Giant golden stones also begin to appear about the same time as the salmonflies, and provide a longer window of "big bug" dry fly fishing, often into July and with some reduction of fishing pressure. If you enjoy less crowded conditions consider early and late season.

Rock Creek enjoys a full season of dry fly action beginning in late March with the skwala stones, and March browns. Cloudy days in April offer excellent baetis hatches, and the summer is rife with salmonflies, giant golden stones, yellow Sallies, spruce moths, terrestrials, and excellent attractor fishing. Baetis return again in the fall, along with great streamer fishing, and the occasional October caddis. Nymph fishing with large black stoneflies such as the Kauffmann's stone #2-4, or the brown stone rubber legs (#8-10) is productive year-round. Nymph fishermen should remember to overweight their flies to get them down deep through the fast pockets of Rock Creek. If in doubt, fish a nymph rig as Rock Creek provides some of the most consistent nymph fishing found in Montana.

Be sure to catch the salmonfly hatch on Rock Creek.
Photo by Brian Grossenbacher.

When to Fish:

Rock Creek fishes well with streamers and nymphs year-round. However, there is consistent dry fly fishing from late March through the middle of summer. If you don't mind crowds, then go for the famous Salmonfly hatch in late May to early June.

Seasons & Limits:

The standard fishing regulations for the *Western* fishing district apply. Please check the *Montana Fishing Regulations and Etiquette* section.

Exceptions to Standard Regulations
From the confluence of the East and West Forks (Near Phillipsburg) to the mouth:

Combined Trout: 3 brown trout daily and in possession, none over 12 inches. Catch-and-release for rainbow trout and cutthroat trout.

Artificial lures only, except anglers 14 years of age and younger may use bait.

Extended season for whitefish and catch-and-release for trout open December 1 to third Saturday in May with artificial lures and/or maggots only.

Closed to fishing from boats July 1 through November 30.

Nearby Fly Fishing:

Clark Fork, Bitterroot, Blackfoot.

Accommodations & Services:

Rock Creek Fisherman's Mercantile & Motel (406-825-6440: www.rcmerc.com) offers two cabins and a six-room hotel, plus fly fishing expertise to boot.

Although the name may fool you, the Big Horn B&B (406-859-3109: www.bighornmontana.com) is located on Rock Creek and also offers a private cabin a short drive from Philipsburg.

There are multiple camping sites all along Rock Creek, including Norton, Grizzly, Dalles, Harry's Flat, Bitterroot Flat, Siria, and Squaw Rock.

Rating: 9

Rock Creek is Western Montana's quintessential freestone trout stream and is hands-down the most consistent nymph fishery in the area year-round. Rock Creek also offers excellent streamer fishing throughout the year. Add to that an exceptional dry fly season in June/July, a noticeable lack of development, and frequent sightings of bighorn sheep, elk, deer, moose, and even black bear and mountain lion, and you'll understand why Rock Creek offers a true Montana flyfishing experience.

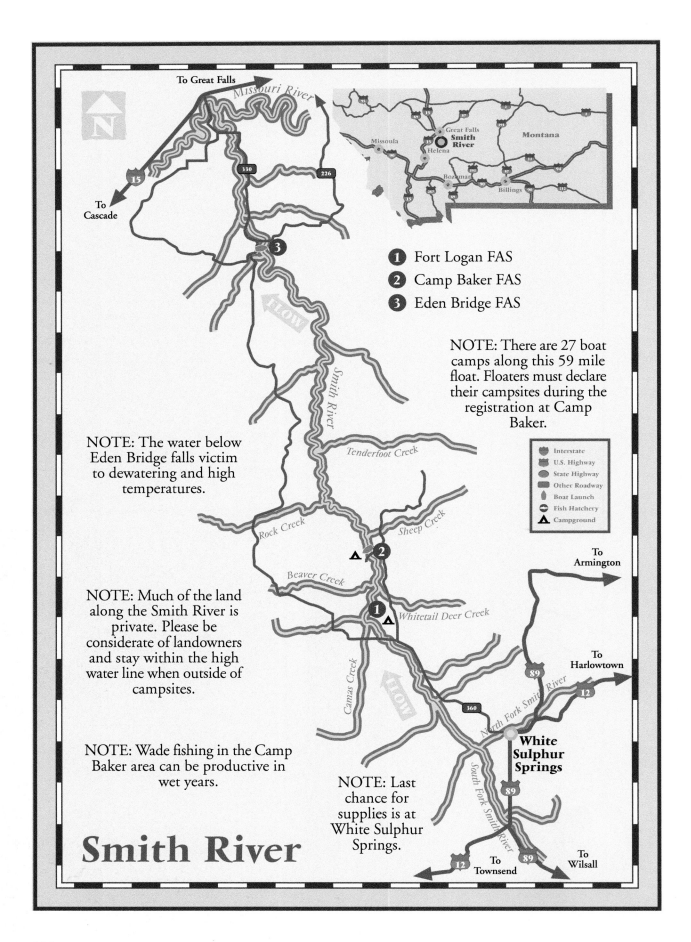

To Great Falls

Missouri River

To Cascade

Smith River

1 Fort Logan FAS
2 Camp Baker FAS
3 Eden Bridge FAS

NOTE: There are 27 boat camps along this 59 mile float. Floaters must declare their campsites during the registration at Camp Baker.

NOTE: The water below Eden Bridge falls victim to dewatering and high temperatures.

Tenderfoot Creek

Rock Creek

Sheep Creek

Beaver Creek

NOTE: Much of the land along the Smith River is private. Please be considerate of landowners and stay within the high water line when outside of campsites.

Whitetail Deer Creek

To Armington

To Harlowtown

Camas Creek

North Fork Smith River

NOTE: Wade fishing in the Camp Baker area can be productive in wet years.

White Sulphur Springs

NOTE: Last chance for supplies is at White Sulphur Springs.

South Fork Smith River

To Townsend

To Wilsall

Interstate
U.S. Highway
State Highway
Other Roadway
Boat Launch
Fish Hatchery
Campground

Missoula
Great Falls
Smith River
Helena
Montana
Bozeman
Billings

Smith River

Smith River

The Smith River runs 121 miles from the town of White Sulphur Springs to the confluence with the Missouri near the town of Ulm. By far the most popular section of the Smith is the 59 mile canyon section that begins at Camp Baker and terminates at Eden Bridge. This magical float twists and turns off the beaten path with limestone cliffs rising 500 feet above the water. Access is limited to 9 parties per day for those fortunate to draw permits in a lottery-type drawing that takes place annually in February. For more information on obtaining permits contact the Montana Fish Wildlife and Parks Great Falls Office at (406) 454-5840. The float season typically extends from mid-April through July 4th and some years again in September, but is heavily dependent upon snow pack, rainfall and irrigation use. Call ahead for stream flows and current conditions (406) 547-3893, or go to the Realtime Stream Flow Table on the Montana USGS website. The Montana Fish Wildlife and Parks has established the following minimum flow guidelines for types of watercraft when floating the Smith.

Driftboats	> 350 CFS
Rafts	> 250 CFS
Canoes	> 150 CFS

Types of Fish:
Brown, Rainbow, and Brook Trout, Whitefish.

Known Hatches:
April-October: Midges.
April: Skwalas.
April-Late May: Baetis.
May-early June: Salmonflies.
May-September: Caddis; Hoppers; Ants; Beetles.
June-Mid August: Golden Stones; Yellow Sallies.
Late June-late August: PMDs.

Equipment to Use:
Rods: 4-5 weight, 8½-9 feet in length.
Lines: Floating line to match rod weight.
Leaders: 9' 4-5x for dries, 7½' 3x for nymphs, 7½' 0-2x for streamers.
Wading: Wet wading possible. Waist-high waders recommended during cooler weather.

Flies to Use:
Dries: Griffith's Gnat #18-22, Parachute Adams #16-20, Olive Sparkle Dun #16-20, RS-2 #16-20, Rusty Spinner #16-22, Stimulator #4-14, Parachute Stone #8-12, Elk Hair Caddis #12-18, Goddard Caddis #12-18, X-Caddis #12-18, Parachute Hopper #8-10, Dave's Hopper #8-10, PMX #8-12, Royal Wulff #10-14, Royal Trude #10-14.
Nymphs: Serendipity #16-22, Brassie #18-22, Pheasant Tail #16-20, Brook's Stonefly Nymph #6-16, Bullethead Skwala #10-12, Kaufmann's Stone #2-8, Bitch Creek #2-8, Sparkle pupa #12-20, Hare's Ear #12-18, Poxyback Stone Nymph #6-18, San Juan Worm #10-18, Prince #12-16, Copper John #12-18, Lightning Bug #14-20.
Streamers: Woolly Bugger #2-8, JJ Special #2-8, Sculpin #2-8.

Cale Van Velkinburgh enjoys a fall day on the upper reaches of the Smith River.
Photo by Brian Grossenbacher.

Overlooking the river at Smith River access.
Photo by Brian Grossenbacher.

On average, the 59-mile trip takes four days to float, and camping must take place in the 27 established boat camps along the river. Floaters must declare their campsites prior to floating the Smith River during the registration process at Camp Baker.

A detailed copy of the Smith River Special Use Area Rules can be obtained at the Montana Fish Wildlife and Parks website or by calling (406) 454-5840.

If this sounds like a lot of red tape just to go for a camping and fishing trip, you may be correct, but then again the greatest things in life do not come easily. The Smith River is a limited resource that demands protection and limited pressure. By controlling the number of launches per day, the Smith River experience is enhanced on multiple levels. Fishing pressure is limited. Crowding is minimal and floaters are able to experience the Smith River in a true wilderness setting…and wild it is.

Floaters should be prepared for rapidly changing weather conditions including snow during the entire floating season. The Smith River flows through a remote and steep canyon, and services are not available between Camp Baker and the Eden Bridge.

Floaters should pack all necessary equipment, food and drinking water for the entire 59-mile trip.

Anglers wanting to experience the Smith without a permit or the four-day investment, can gain access at Camp Baker and wade up or downstream. Anglers wishing to float the Smith can put in nine miles upstream and float down to Camp Baker when conditions permit. The fishing below Eden Bridge diminishes due to irrigation draws, and high temperatures.

The fish on the Smith are not particularly picky and will rise enthusiastically to well presented attractor dries, caddis patterns, and later in the season, grasshoppers. The Smith enjoys a wonderful salmonfly hatch between mid-May and early June where large bitch creek nymphs and Kaufmann stones work well fished in the deep pools. Once the adult flies emerge, try the Turck's tarantula #2-6, Kaufmann's stimulator #2-6 or the Rainy's foam gorilla stonefly.

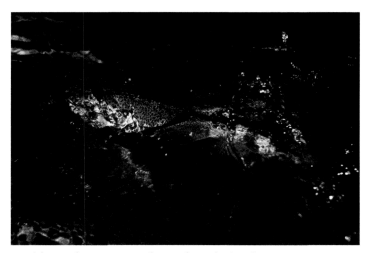

Healthy rainbows are a regular catch on the Smith.
Photo by Brian Grossenbacher.

When to Fish:

Timing is everything on the Smith, and unfortunately flow conditions are not always predictable. The main float season is from April to early-July. Although fun for floating, the high and dirty waters of runoff, typically in May, are debilitating to the angler. Mid- to late-April can offer great fishing, but weather is unpredictable, as is early runoff. Early-June should offer solid fishing, but once again, if runoff is late or long, fishing will be hampered.

Seasons & Limits:

The standard fishing regulations for the *Central* fishing district apply. Please check the *Montana Fishing Regulations and Etiquette* section.

Exceptions to Standard Regulations

Applies to entire water body:

Floating on the Smith River between Camp Baker and Eden Bridge is strictly limited. Mandatory registration, floater's fee and other regulations apply. A drawing for launch dates is held in February with remaining launches filled on a first-come basis. Contact the Great Falls FWP office at 406-454-5840 for more information.

Downstream from confluence of North and South Forks:

Open entire year.

Camp Baker Bridge to Eden Bridge (Huntsberger Bridge)

Artificial lures only, except anglers 14 years of age and younger may use bait.

Combined Trout: 3 under 13 inches daily and in possession and 1 over 22 inches daily and in possession.

Nearby Fly Fishing:

Missouri River, Sheep Creek.

Accommodations & Services:

Count on a bare minimum of three nights, four days to float the river. Designated campgrounds are the only option on the permit portion of the river. Before putting in at Camp Baker, White Sulpher Springs is the closest town for lodging (Grassy Mt. Lodge, 406-547-3357: www.grassymountain.com, Spa Hot Springs, 406-547-3366: www.spahotsprings.com). When taking out at Eden Bridge, Great Falls offers the typical big city options (Hampton Inn 406-426-7866, Fairfield Inn 800-228-2800, Holiday Inn 406-455-1000, etc.). Outfitters on the Smith River include Paul Roos Outfitters (406-442-5489, 800-858-3497: www.paulroosoutfitters.com) and Montana River Outfitters (406-761-1677: www.montanariveroutfitters.com) amongst a handful of others.

Rating: 8.5

The Smith is arguably as close to the fabled "Montana experience" as you can get. As such, it is extremely difficult to get a float permit for the 60-mile canyon stretch between Camp Baker and Eden Bridge. Every year, thousands of anglers and floaters alike submit for a limited number of permits with less than 10% succeeding. Only nine float parties are allowed to leave per day, although Smith River outfitters can offer additional opportunities. The Smith offers stunning vistas around every bend, and good shots at large browns and rainbows.

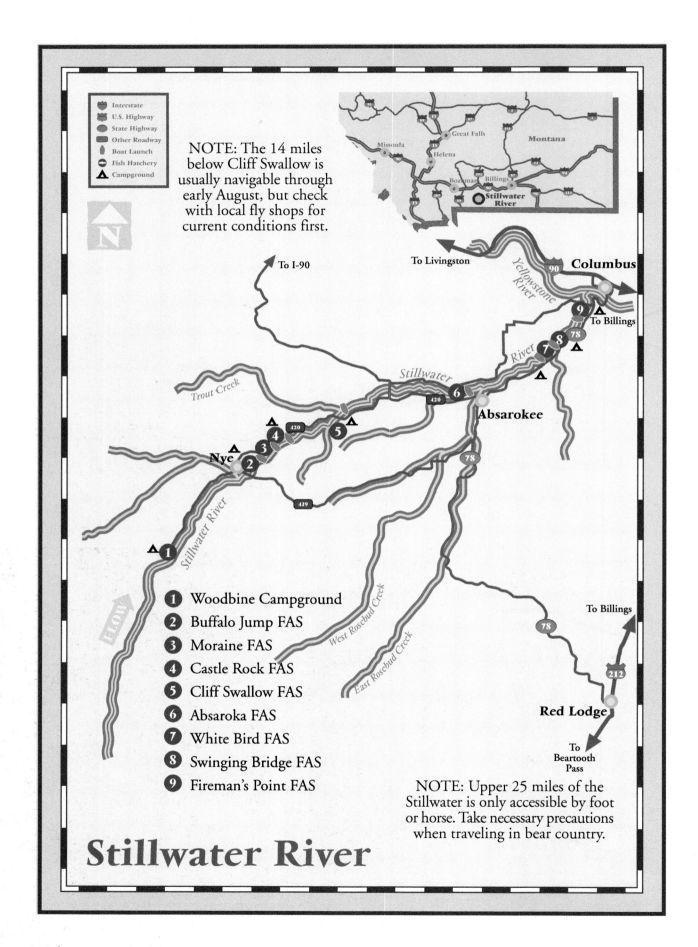

NOTE: The 14 miles below Cliff Swallow is usually navigable through early August, but check with local fly shops for current conditions first.

Legend:
- Interstate
- U.S. Highway
- State Highway
- Other Roadway
- Boat Launch
- Fish Hatchery
- Campground

To I-90

To Livingston

To Billings

Columbus

Absarokee

Nye

Trout Creek

Stillwater

Yellowstone River

River

Stillwater River

West Rosebud Creek

East Rosebud Creek

To Billings

Red Lodge

To Beartooth Pass

1 Woodbine Campground
2 Buffalo Jump FAS
3 Moraine FAS
4 Castle Rock FAS
5 Cliff Swallow FAS
6 Absaroka FAS
7 White Bird FAS
8 Swinging Bridge FAS
9 Fireman's Point FAS

NOTE: Upper 25 miles of the Stillwater is only accessible by foot or horse. Take necessary precautions when traveling in bear country.

Stillwater River

Montana
Missoula
Great Falls
Helena
Bozeman   Billings
Stillwater River

FLOW

Stillwater River

Just as Greenland and Iceland share names with polar opposite descriptors, so does the Stillwater enjoy its ironic namesake. There is nothing still about the water that pours out of the east side of the Beartooth Mountains. The 65+ miles of the Stillwater are fast enough to make the upper Madison and its 50-mile riffle blush. In fact, whitewater enthusiasts are becoming quite a presence on the river, especially in the early summer in the faster sections above Nye. As for the fishing, the Stillwater is floatable in the early season from Nye down to Columbus, where it joins the Yellowstone. After early August only the final 14 miles below the Cliff Swallow access are navigable, and even then it becomes bony enough for only the most experienced oarsman. Do not attempt the Stillwater in a hard-sided boat unless you are looking to close out your insurance policy or attempting to give your boat a proper burial at sea. Rafts are the preferred mode of transport, and wading anglers will enjoy the multitude of public access points with excellent camping as well. The Stillwater is not a destination river by size, but is a formidable fishery in between the Bighorn and Yellowstone waters for the traveling angler. Spend a day on the Stillwater during your next trip west and we bet it will become a traditional stopping point on your future fishing excursions.

Types of Fish:
Rainbow, Brown, Cutthroat, and Brook Trout.

Known Hatches:
January-March: Midges.
Late February-Early March: Black Stoneflies.
Late-April: Blue-Winged Olives, March Browns, Caddis.
June: Golden Stones, Yellow Sallies.
Mid-July-August: Caddis, PMDs, Brown Drakes, Hoppers.

Equipment to Use:
Rods: 4-6 weight, 8-9 feet in length.
Lines: Floating line for dries and nymphs.
Leaders: 9' 5x for dries, 7½' 3x for bigger nymphs, 4x for smaller nymphs.
Wading: Chest-high waders with felt-soled boots for most of season. Wading can be tricky due to swift current and numerous boulders. Some wet-wading may be possible in late-July and August.

Flies to Use:
Dries: Griffith's Gnat #20-22, Red Quill #12-16, Parachute Adams #16-20, Rusty Spinner #16-22, Olive Sparkle Dun #16-20, Elk Hair Caddis #14-16, Goddard Caddis #12-16, Stimulator #8-10, Yellow Sally #14-16, Royal Trude #12-16, Hoppers #6-12, Beetles #14-18, Ants #10-20.
Nymphs: Serendipty #16-22, Brassie #18-22, Pheasant Tail #16-18, Hare's Ear #12-16, Sparkle Pupa #14-16, Kaufmann's Golden Stone #8-12, Brown Rubber Legs #8-12, Copper John #12-18, Prince #12-18, Lightning Bug #14-18.
Streamers: Muddler Minnow #2-8, Woolly Bugger #4-8, Sculpin #2-8.

Jenny mending on the not-so-Stillwater.
Photo by Brian Grossenbacher

Dusk on the Stillwater.
Photo by Brian Grossenbacher.

Learning from a great teacher.
Photo by Brian Grossenbacher.

When to Fish:

The Stillwater fishes well year-round. Winter fishing is consistent with frequent midge hatches. Spring and early summer offer several hatches, including baetis and caddis. Runoff typically arrives in late May to early June, and sometimes lasts into early July. Mid to late summer brings great hopper fishing and other terrestrial activity. Fall can be even better, with the browns from the Yellowstone moving up in the tributaries.

Seasons & Limits:

The standard fishing regulations for the *Central* fishing district apply. Please check the *Montana Fishing Regulations and Etiquette* section.
Exceptions to Standard Regulations
Applies to entire water body:
  Open entire year. Combined Trout: 2 daily and in possession, only 1 over 13 inches.

Nearby Fly Fishing:

Big Horn, Yellowstone, Clark's Fork of the Yellowstone, Rosebud Creek, West Fork Stillwater, high alpine lakes: Mystic, West Rosebud and Emerald Lakes.

Accommodations & Services:

Several B&Bs and rental cabins are available, including Lena's Cabins (406-328-6248) just three miles out of Absarokee, and The Stillwater Lodge (406-328-4899) on the main road in Absarokee. In Columbus, there's a Super 8 Motel (406-322-4101) and the Riverside Guest Cabins (406-322-5066). There are a handful of restaurants, most notably, the Rosebud Café (406-328-6969), the Stake-Out (406-328-6566) and the Dew Drop Inn Old Fashioned Hamburger Stand (406-328-4121). A couple of camping sites are available on the lower stretch of the Stillwater River, including the Forest Service accesses of Swinging Bridge and Whitebird.

Rating: 8

The proximity to Bighorn and Yellowstone, the probability of several 14-18" trout, good access, an off-the-beaten-path location, and the feel of Montana 50 years ago, make this sleeper river a strong 8.

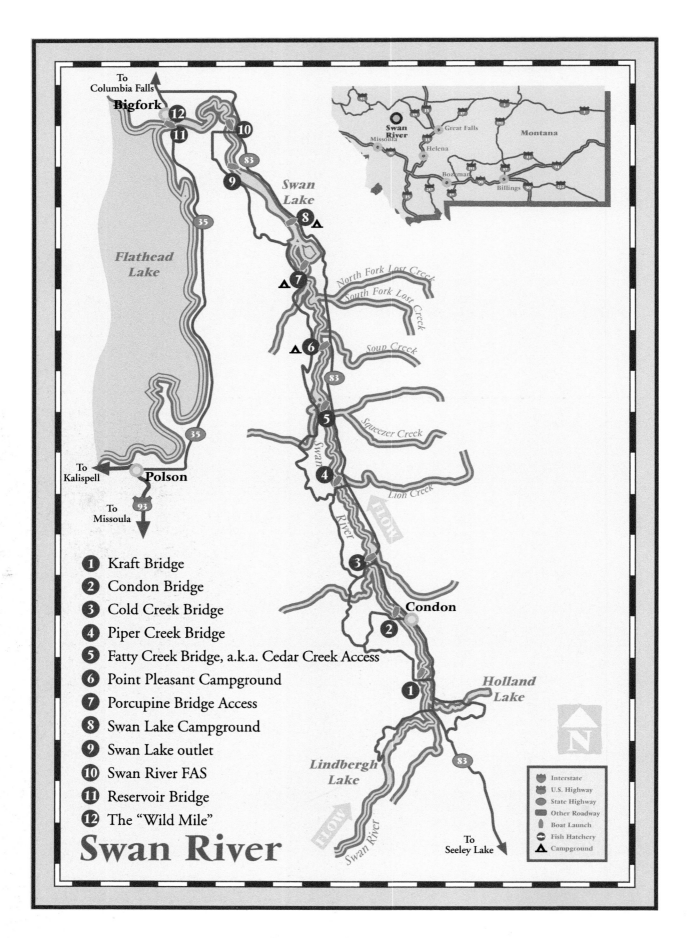

1 Kraft Bridge
2 Condon Bridge
3 Cold Creek Bridge
4 Piper Creek Bridge
5 Fatty Creek Bridge, a.k.a. Cedar Creek Access
6 Point Pleasant Campground
7 Porcupine Bridge Access
8 Swan Lake Campground
9 Swan Lake outlet
10 Swan River FAS
11 Reservoir Bridge
12 The "Wild Mile"

Swan River

Swan River

The Swan River begins high in the Mission Mountains, twisting and turning through verdant forests, magnificent vistas, and some of Montana's most rugged country. The entire river system is just under 100 miles long including lakes, but most anglers concentrate on the 60-mile stretch from Lindbergh Lake to Swan Lake.

The unique nature of the Swan presents anglers with an interesting conundrum—row versus wade? Wade fishing is difficult due to the deep pools, downed trees, and voracious mosquitoes. Float fishing is tricky due to the swift currents, braided channels, blind corners and treacherous log jams. For all of the reasons mentioned above, the Swan does not receive a tremendous amount of fishing pressure. For those willing to brave the elements, you will find a generous selection of 8"-12" trout, with a handful of larger fish thrown in for good measure. The Swan enjoys a dynamic cross section of fish species. Rainbow and native cutthroat trout are most prevalent, but you may also see brook and bull trout, northern pike, largemouth bass, and lake trout.

Types of Fish:
Westslope Cutthroat, Rainbow, Bull and Brook Trout, Pike, Whitefish.

Known Hatches:
May-June: Caddis.
June: Caddis, Yellow Sallies, Golden Stones.
July-August: Hoppers, Caddis, PMDs.

Equipment to Use:
Rods: 4-6 weight, 8½-9 feet in length.
Lines: Weight forward floating for dry fly and nymph fishing.
Leaders: 7½' 3-4x nymphing, 9' 4-5x for dries, 7' 1x-2x for streamers.
Wading: Chest-high waders are recommended.

Flies to Use:
Dries: Humpies #12-16, Royal Wulff #12-16, Royal Trude #12-16, Parachute Adams #12-16, Parachute Hopper #10, Elk Hair Caddis #14-16.
Nymphs: Pheasant Tail Nymph #12-16, Beadhead Copper John #12-16, Lightning Bug #14-16, Hare's Ear #12-16.
Streamers: Woolly Bugger #2-8.

Brian Grossenbacher enjoying an afternoon alone on the Swan.
Photo by Brian Grossenbacher.

Mackenzie Grossenbacher hooks up on the Swan.
Photo by Jenny Grossenbacher.

The Swan parallels Highway 83 for much of its length, with generous access via logging roads and well-maintained campgrounds. Floating above Cold Creek Bridge is not recommended in anything larger than a canoe due to the aforementioned challenges. Floaters should check in at Condon or Big Fork for updated river conditions and may consider bringing an ax or saw in the event of impassible log jams. The water below Porcupine Bridge slows down considerably, allowing for more time fishing and less time navigating. It should be noted that the take-out at the Swan Lake campground requires a one-mile paddle across the lake.

Below the outlet of Swan Lake the river widens and slows considerably. Anglers can put in at the Montana Highway 209 Bridge east of Ferndale for an eight-mile float to the Swan River Road Bridge. This tranquil section may become too warm in the summer for trout, but the backwaters maintain a healthy population of northern pike. The Swan finishes strong and fast below the Big Fork dam before it empties into Flathead Lake. In a one-mile stretch aptly named, "The Wild Mile," the river drops 100 feet and its Class IV and V whitewater is a popular destination for expert kayakers.

The fish on the Swan are not discerning, and general attractor patterns such as humpies, PMX's, stimulators and parachute Adams will suffice nicely. The Swan enjoys a prolific yellow Sally hatch early in the summer from run-off through mid-July, and hopper patterns will take you through September. Bigger fish on the Swan will hold in the cover of log jams and are not shy about taking large nymphs and streamers. The Swan enjoys a tantalizing population of large bull trout, however current regulations prohibit purposely fishing for them. If you happen to catch a bull trout, release it carefully and quickly to help preserve this threatened species.

Rainbow before release. Photo by Brian Grossenbacher.

Dry fly fishing for cutthroats yields its rewards. Photo by Brian Grossenbacher.

When to Fish:
Early to mid summer offers easy dry fly fishing with just about any attractor pattern.

Seasons & Limits:
The standard fishing regulations for the *Western* fishing district apply. Please check the *Montana Fishing Regulations and Etiquette* section.
Exceptions to Standard Regulations
Piper Creek Bridge downstream to Swan Lake
    Catch-and-release for cutthroat trout and rainbow trout. Artificial lures only.
Swan Lake downstream to the Highway 35 Bridge
    Open entire year. Catch-and-release for cutthroat trout.

Nearby Fly Fishing:
South Fork of the Flathead, Flathead Lake, Swan Lake, Clearwater River.

Accommodations & Services:
In Condon, try the Holland Lake Lodge (406 754-2282: www.hollandlakelodge.com) for an authentic Western resort in a beautiful setting. Seely Lake offers numerous options, including the backcountry trip of a lifetime with the Bob Marshall Wilderness Ranch (406-754-2285: www.wildernessranch.com).

Rating: 7
For ease of fishing and beauty, the Swan River ranks right up there. Don't even bother taking your small flies—the fish aren't too picky and just about any attractor pattern will do the trick. Add to that the lack of crowds, and the Swan is definitely worth a trip.

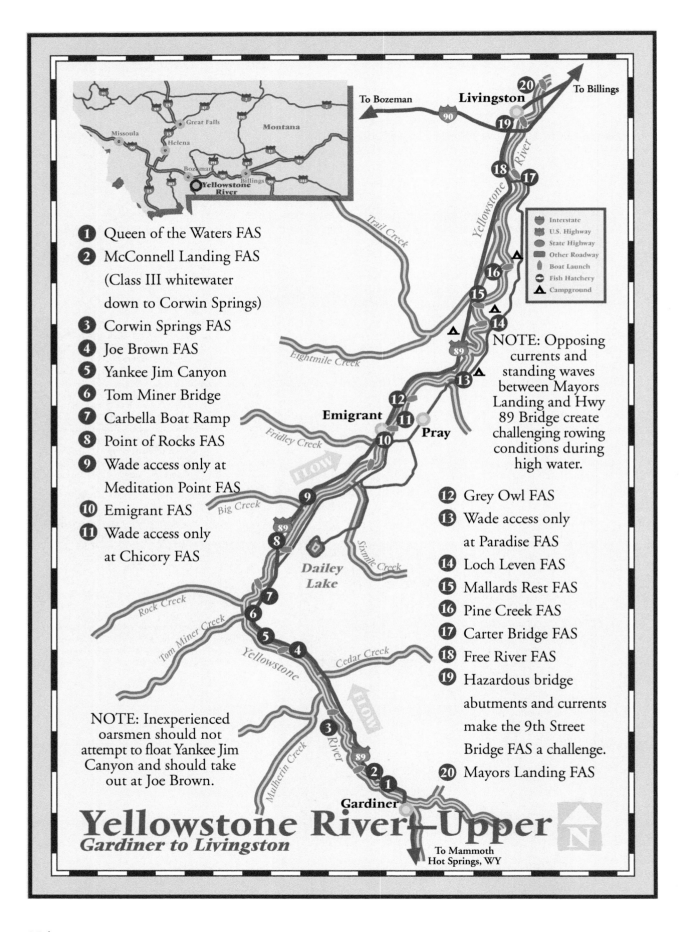

1 Queen of the Waters FAS
2 McConnell Landing FAS
(Class III whitewater
down to Corwin Springs)
3 Corwin Springs FAS
4 Joe Brown FAS
5 Yankee Jim Canyon
6 Tom Miner Bridge
7 Carbella Boat Ramp
8 Point of Rocks FAS
9 Wade access only at
Meditation Point FAS
10 Emigrant FAS
11 Wade access only
at Chicory FAS

12 Grey Owl FAS
13 Wade access only
at Paradise FAS
14 Loch Leven FAS
15 Mallards Rest FAS
16 Pine Creek FAS
17 Carter Bridge FAS
18 Free River FAS
19 Hazardous bridge
abutments and currents
make the 9th Street
Bridge FAS a challenge.
20 Mayors Landing FAS

NOTE: Opposing currents and standing waves between Mayors Landing and Hwy 89 Bridge create challenging rowing conditions during high water.

NOTE: Inexperienced oarsmen should not attempt to float Yankee Jim Canyon and should take out at Joe Brown.

To Bozeman   Livingston   To Billings

Emigrant   Pray

Dailey Lake

Gardiner

To Mammoth Hot Springs, WY

Legend:
Interstate
U.S. Highway
State Highway
Other Roadway
Boat Launch
Fish Hatchery
Campground

Yellowstone River—Upper
Gardiner to Livingston

N

Yellowstone River
Gardiner to Livingston

The longest free-flowing river in the lower 48 states, the Yellowstone River begins high in the snow-capped mountains of Wyoming. After a tumultuous journey through Yellowstone National Park, the celebrated, yet more forgiving Paradise Valley, and the flatlands of central and eastern Montana, the Yellowstone only offers its fruitful waters to the Missouri after finally crossing the North Dakota border. This tri-state journey traverses some 672 miles through deep canyons, mountain valleys, vast cottonwood groves and prairie grasslands.

The blue-ribbon portion of the Yellowstone River is found between Gardiner and Big Timber, Montana covering 100+ miles. This section is not wader friendly by its nature. It is deep and swift, and the rocky bottom is akin to walking on greased bowling balls. Public access is limited to maintained fishing access sites, yet luckily for the angler, these sites are seldom more than six miles apart.

From the town of Gardiner to the Carbella access, the

Jimmy Kloote and friend enjoy a productive day of fishing on the upper Yellowstone.
Photo by Brian Grossenbacher.

Types of Fish:
Yellowstone Cutthroat, Brown, and Rainbow Trout, Whitefish.

Known Hatches:
Mid March-Late April: Baetis, Midges.
Late April-Mid May: Caddis. Early June-mid July: Salmonflies, Golden Stones, Caddis.
July-August: PMDs, Yellow Sallies, Hoppers, Caddis, Tricos, Green Drake, Nocturnal Stone.
Mid September-Mid October: Baetis.

Equipment to Use:
Rods: 5-7 weight, 8½-9 feet in length.
Lines: Floating line for dries and nymphs, sink tip for streamers.
Leaders: 9' 3-6x for dries, 7½' 3x for nymphs, 7' 0-2x for streamers.
Wading: Deep river (30'+), mostly floating. Wet wade riffles in late summer.

Flies to Use:
Dries: Parachute Adams #12-22, BWO #18-20, Goddard's Caddis #14-18, Black Caddis #18-20, Elk Hair Caddis #14-18, X Caddis #14-18, PMX #8-12, Parachute Hopper #4-10, Chernobyl Ant/Hopper #4-8, Rainy's Hopper #6-10, Royal Wulff #10-14, Royal Trude #12-16.
Nymphs: Sparkle Pupa #18-20, Copper John #12-18, Green & Brown Bugger #4-6, Prince Nymph #12-16, Pheasant Tail #12-18, Lightning Bug #14-18, Yellow Prince #12-18, Hare's Ear #12-18, Girdle Bug #6-8, Anderson's Brown Stone #6-8.
Streamers: Green, Brown or Black Bugger #2-6, White, Natural or Green Zonker #2-6, JJ's Special #2-4, Double Bunny Leech #2-4, Conehead Buggers #2-6, Bow River Bugger #4-6.

When to Fish:
The Yellowstone is prime in April and early-May before run off. Great baetis fishing is the norm from late March through April and, in a lucky year, if runoff is late, you can hit the amazing Mother's Day caddis hatch from late April to early May. If runoff is short, you may be lucky enough to get into a great salmonfly hatch in mid to late June. It's especially good the farther up (south) the river you go. July and August can bring unbelievable hopper action. Late July through August is the best time for fair-weather fishermen, due to warm weather. September brings continued hopper action and the return of Baetis. Fishing remains strong through late October, with both baetis and streamer fishing.

The Absaroka Mountains offer a stunning backdrop for the Yellowstone River. Photo by Jenny Grossenbacher.

Yellowstone river flows impatiently, and violently at times. Floaters must use caution on this stretch, and all but the most advanced whitewater experts should avoid floating Yankee Jim Canyon. We also recommend floating this section in a raft rather than a hard sided boat, as robust suck holes, and SUV-sized boulders litter the river's course. In spite of the challenging floating conditions, anglers are frequently rewarded in the upper river by vibrantly-colored cutthroat that rise to the fly with a painfully-slow, open-mouthed gape. The unhurried take of the cutthroat often has anglers setting the hook well before the fish takes the fly. If you do time the hook set just right, remember that the Yellowstone cutthroat trout is classified as a *Montana Species of Concern* and is protected by catch and release regulations.

Downstream from Carbella the Yellowstone mellows substantially, and the willow-lined banks open to stunning views of the Absaroka mountains, named after the Crow Indian word for blackbird. This section of the Yellowstone has been dubbed the "Paradise Valley". The surrounding mountain vistas and fertile valley floor effortlessly live up to the name. Around Pine Creek the river gains momentum and churns its way hastily towards Livingston with more prolific riffles, runs, twists and turns. The water through this section regularly produces healthy-sized browns and rainbows averaging 14"-16", with several larger trout as well, and a smaller number of decent-sized cutthroat in the 10"-14" range. Although floating is still the preferred way to fish this section, there are excellent opportunities throughout this stretch to get out of the boat and wade-fish numerous productive riffles and runs.

Blankets of caddis are common during the famous Mother's Day caddis hatch on the Yellowstone. Photo by Brian Grossenbacher.

Seasons & Limits:

The standard fishing regulations for the *Central* and *Eastern* fishing districts apply. Please check the *Montana Fishing Regulations and Etiquette* section.
Exceptions to Standard Regulations
Yellowstone National Park Boundary to I-90 Bridge at Billings
   Open entire year.
Yellowstone National Park boundary to Highway 78 Bridge at Columbus
   Catch-and-release for cutthroat trout.
Emigrant Bridge to Pine Creek Bridge
   Combined Trout: 5 brown and/or rainbow trout daily and in possession, includes 4 under 13 inches and 1 over 22 inches. Artificial lures only, except anglers 14 years of age and younger may use bait.
   Extended season for whitefish and catch-and-release for trout open December 1 to third Saturday in May with artificial lures and/or maggots only.

Nearby Fly Fishing:

Yellowstone National Park, Madison, Gallatin, Boulder, Paradise Valley Spring Creeks.

Accommodations & Services:

Livingston and Bozeman offer countless options. Below are a few of our favorites in Livingston. See the lower Madison or Gallatin for suggestions for Bozeman.

The Yellowstone House (406-586-1922: www.yellowstonehouse.com) is a lovely riverside cabin with access to the local Chico Hot Springs. It holds 8+ adults, or the Honeymoon Cabin is great for a couple.

For B&Bs, check out Howler's Inn (406-586-0304: www.howlersinn.com). The quaint country setting halfway between Bozeman and Livingston, and the howling wolves, make for a great option.

To follow in the footsteps of Buffalo Bill and Calamity Jane, try a true cowboy hotel right in the heart of Livingston, The Murray Hotel (406-222-1350: www.murrayhotel.com) or the 100+ year old Chico Hot Springs Lodge outside of Emigrant

Several campgrounds are along the river: Paradise, Loch Leven and Mallards Rest, as well as a great KOA right on the Yellowstone at Pine Creek. A couple hundred yards up the road is the tiny town of Pine Creek and a café that has outdoor concerts and BBQs on the weekends in the summer.

For restaurants, don't miss the Rib & Chop House in town. If you are farther south, and in the mood for a 5-star meal, try Chico Hot Springs Lodge (406-333-4933: www.chicohotsprings.com).

Rating: 10!

When it comes to big-river, Western fly fishing, the Yellowstone can't be beat. With a couple hundred plus miles of varied fishing, amazing scenery, a legitimate shot at 20"+ trout, and its free flowing wildness, every serious fly fisher should have the Yellowstone on their must-fish list.

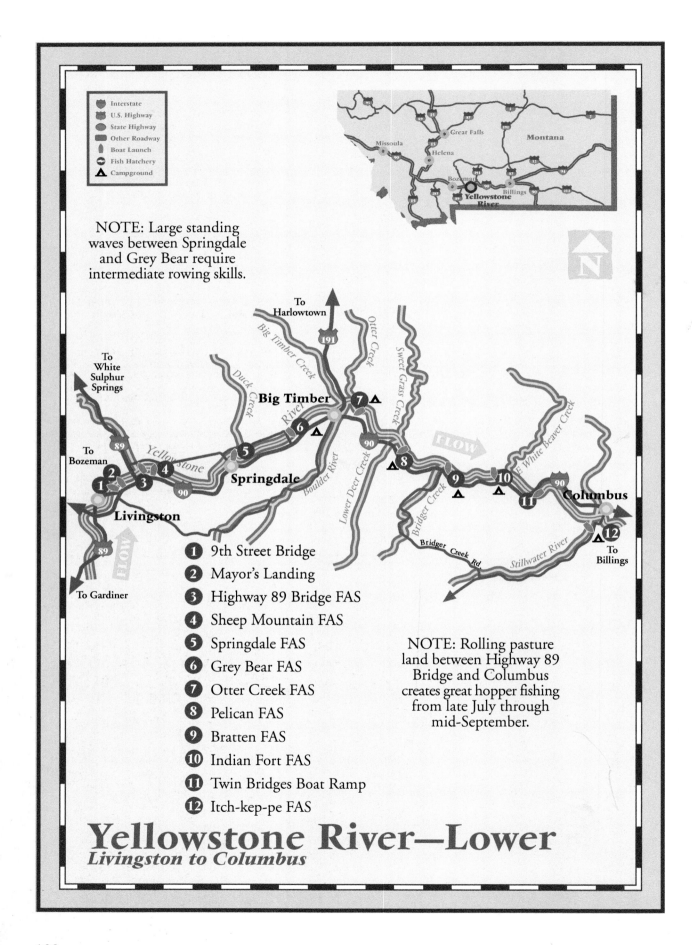

NOTE: Large standing waves between Springdale and Grey Bear require intermediate rowing skills.

NOTE: Rolling pasture land between Highway 89 Bridge and Columbus creates great hopper fishing from late July through mid-September.

Legend:
- Interstate
- U.S. Highway
- State Highway
- Other Roadway
- Boat Launch
- Fish Hatchery
- Campground

1 9th Street Bridge
2 Mayor's Landing
3 Highway 89 Bridge FAS
4 Sheep Mountain FAS
5 Springdale FAS
6 Grey Bear FAS
7 Otter Creek FAS
8 Pelican FAS
9 Bratten FAS
10 Indian Fort FAS
11 Twin Bridges Boat Ramp
12 Itch-kep-pe FAS

Yellowstone River—Lower
Livingston to Columbus

Yellowstone River
Livingston to Columbus

As the river weaves its way under I-90 and through the heart of Livingston, the scenic value decreases somewhat. Thankfully, the inverse is true of the size of the fish in this section, with consistent fishing throughout the year for large 18"+ browns and rainbows in particular. Floaters, beware of the 9th Street Bridge—it is low and narrow, and deceptive currents can push you off your mark as you head under the bridge.

North of Livingston the scenery improves again, with views of the distant Crazy Mountains and the rugged cliffs around Sheep Mountain. Nutrient-rich springs between Livingston and Columbus consistently maintain a healthy temperature for trout throughout the summer season. The river slows and the opportunity for even larger 20+ inch trout becomes more likely, although the number of fish declines slightly.

Downstream of Columbus the river widens, the current slows, and the water temperatures warm up. There are opportunities to catch smallmouth, walleye, carp, catfish, burbot, and even paddlefish in these lower reaches.

Regardless of which section you fish, you'll find that the Yellowstone River is the quintessential Western, big-water, trout river. The season starts off with a bang with fantastic baetis fishing in April, right into the Mother's Day caddis hatch in early May. From there, depending on the timing of runoff, you may have the opportunity to fish the salmon fly hatch or, better yet, head out a little later in the summer for memorable hopper fishing. Throughout most of its course, the banks of the Yellowstone are lined with lush, irrigated hay fields, and from late-July through mid-September, unsuspecting hoppers

Types of Fish:
Yellowstone Cutthroat, Brown, and Rainbow Trout, Carp, Whitefish.

Known Hatches:
Mid March-Late April: Baetis, Midges.
Late April-Mid May: Caddis.
Early June-mid July: Salmonflies, Golden Stones, Caddis.
July-August: PMDs, Yellow Sallies, Hoppers, Caddis, Tricos, Green Drake, Nocturnal Stone.
Mid September-Mid October: Baetis.

Equipment to Use:
Rods: 5-7 weight, 8½-9 feet in length.
Lines: Floating line for dries and nymphs, sink tip for streamers.
Leaders: 9' 3-6x for dries, 7½' 3x for nymphs, 7' 0-2x for streamers.
Wading: Deep river (30'+ at points), mostly floating, wet wade riffles in late summer, otherwise you'll need full waders, unless exclusively float fishing.

Flies to Use:
Dries: Parachute Adams #12-22, BWO #18-20, Goddard's Caddis #14-18, Black Caddis #18-20, Elk Hair Caddis #14-18, X Caddis #14-18, PMX #8-12, Parachute Hopper #4-10, Chernobyl Ant/Hopper #4-8, Grand Hopper #6-10, Royal Wulff #10-14, Royal Trude #12-16.
Nymphs: Sparkle Pupa #18-20, Copper John #12-18, Green & Brown Bugger #4-6, Prince Nymph #12-16, Pheasant Tail #12-18, Lightning Bug #14-18, Yellow Prince #12-18, Hare's Ear #12-18, Girdle Bug #6-8, Anderson's Brown Stone #6-8.
Streamers: Green, Brown or Black Bugger #2-6, White, Natural or Green Zonker #2-6, JJ's Special #2-4, Double Bunny Leech #2-4, Conehead Buggers #2-6, Bow River Bugger #4-6.

Wet wading is possible in some areas in late summer.
Photo by Brian Grossenbacher.

A drift boat is the best way to explore the variety of waters the Yellowstone has to offer. Photo by Brian Grossenbacher.

are regularly blown into the water and into the waiting craws of predatory trout. Few things in life are more exciting than watching a hopper pattern disappear into the explosion of an aggressive trout take. Hopper fishing segues into fall baetis and the season wraps up with productive streamer fishing in October and November.

Make sure to bring your camera along, not only to capture the stunning views and pictures of healthy wild trout, but also for the wildlife. There are frequent sightings of bald eagle, deer, elk, black bear, and even otter, throughout the length of the river

Handling a nice rainbow in a catch and release net.
Photo by Brian Grossenbacher.

When to Fish:

The Yellowstone is at its prime in April and early-May, before runoff. Great baetis fishing is the norm from late-March through April, and if runoff is late you can hit the amazing Mother's Day caddis hatch from late April to early May. If runoff is short, you may be lucky enough to get into a great salmonfly hatch in mid- to late-June. It's especially good the farther up (south) the river you go. July and August can bring unbelievable hopper action. Late July through August is the best time for fair-weather fishermen, due to predictably-warm weather. September brings continued hopper action and the return of baetis. The fishing remains strong through late October, with both baetis and streamer fishing.

Seasons & Limits:

The standard fishing regulations for the *Central, Eastern* and *National Park Service* fishing districts apply. Please check the *Montana Fishing Regulations and Etiquette* section.
Exceptions to Standard Regulations
Yellowstone National Park Boundary to I-90 Bridge at Billings
　Open entire year.
Yellowstone National Park boundary to Highway 78 Bridge at Columbus
　Catch-and-release for cutthroat trout.

Nearby Fly Fishing:

Boulder, Paradise Valley Spring Creeks, Stillwater River, Gallatin.

Accommodations & Services:

If you want to follow in the footsteps of Buffalo Bill and Calamity Jane, try a true cowboy hotel, The Murray Hotel (406-222-1350: www.murrayhotel.com). For dinner, don't miss the Rib & Chop House in town.

If you are farther east, try the Grand Hotel in Big Timber (406-932-4459: www.thegrand-hotel.com) for both lodging and a fantastic dinner.

There are a few campgrounds along the river, including Sheep Mountain, Spring Dale and Indian Fort.

Rating: 8

The lower stretches of the Yellowstone hold fewer but even larger trout. The stretch from Hwy. 89 down to Pelican is more popular than the lower reaches. There are beautiful cliffs and slower, flatter water in the lower stretch. One of the drawbacks is that power boats are sometimes seen the farther northeast you go.

Hard core anglers can get their winter fix on the spring creeks.
Photo by Brian Grossenbacher.

Traveling in Bear Country

Many of the streams and rivers in Montana flow through bear country. Most fishermen never see a bear, but measures should be taken to learn about the special precautions for traveling in bear country.

IMPORTANT CAUTION: Bears are unpredictable and wild animals. Although the precautions discussed below are recommended by many experienced outdoorsmen, these precautions cannot guarantee your safe travel in bear country or eliminate all risks of injury or death. You are always at risk when you make the decision to fish in bear country.

Avoid Surprising Bears
- Make plenty of noise to let bears know you are coming. Bears will typically make efforts to avoid humans if they know humans are present. Clapping, talking loudly or calling out seems to be more effective than bells.
- Fishermen and hikers should avoid traveling alone in bear country.
- Special attention should be made when fishing streams or hiking in heavy cover where it may be hard for a bear to see, smell or hear your presence.
- Avoid areas of known bear activity such as berry patches, partly consumed animal carcasses, diggings or logs that have been torn apart.

Bear Encounters
- Assume a non-threatening posture and do not look directly at the bear as this may be interpreted as a direct challenge.
- Use a low calm tone of voice or do not talk at all.
- Often times bears will bluff charge but if you are attacked, lie flat on the ground and protect your neck and head with your arms and hands. Remain motionless until you are sure the bear has left the area.

Use of Pepper Spray to deter Bear Attacks
Proper use of pepper spray may be an effective deterrent in the event of a bear attack. Carrying pepper spray should never be a reason to avoid taking necessary precautions when traveling in bear country.

Educate yourself before traveling in bear country.
When hiking or fishing in National Parks or Forests check in with rangers or staff to learn about areas that receive heavy bear activity and obvious signs of bear presence.
- Anglers: Don't leave fish entrails on shorelines of lakes and streams. Sink entrails in deep water. If you don't properly dispose of entrails you increase danger to yourself and to the next person to use the area.
- Campers: Camp away from trails and areas where you see grizzly signs. Keep a clean camp at all times, and avoid cooking smelly foods. Hang all food, trash and other odorous items well away from camp and at least 10 feet above ground and 4 feet from any vertical support, or store in a bear-proof container. Livestock feed should be treated the same as human food. Keep tents and sleeping bags free of odors. If possible, don't sleep in the same clothes you wore while cooking or eating.

Source
Montana Fish Wildlife and Parks Website: http://fwp.mt.gov/wildthings/livingwwildlife/grizzlybears/grizzlycountry.html

Hookup below Carter's Bridge on the Yellowstone.
Photo by Brian Grossenbacher.

Resources

This listing of resources is provided as a courtesy to help you enjoy your travels and fishing experience and is not intended to imply an endorsement of services either by the publisher or author. These listings are as accurate as possible as of the time of publication and are subject to change.

Absarokee

Fish Montana Fly Shop
3 N. Stillwater Rd.
Absorakee, MT 59001
406-328-6548
800-894-2956

Alder

Ruby Springs Lodge
P.O. Box 119
Alder, MT 59710
800-278-7829 (toll free)
www.rubyspringslodge.com

Big Sky

East Slope Anglers
P.O. Box 160249 (Mailing)
47855 Gallatin Rd.
Big Sky, MT 59716
406-995-4369 (local)
888-359-3974 (toll free)
www.eastslopeoutdoors.com

Gallatin River Guides
P.O. Box 160212 (Mailing)
47430 Gallatin Rd.
Big Sky, MT 59716
406-995-2290
888-707-1505 (toll free)
www.montanaflyfishing.com

Lone Mountain Ranch
750 Lone Mountain
Ranch Rd.
Big Sky, MT 59716
800-514-4644
www.lmranch.com

Big Timber

Sweet Cast Angler
P.O. Box 582 (mailing)
115 First Ave. W.
Big Timber, MT 59011
406-932-4469
Email: sweetcast.angler@
yahoo.com

Bigfork

Two River Gear
P.O. Box 591 (mailing)
603 Electric Ave.
Bigfork, MT 59911
406-837-3474
www.tworivergear.net

Billings

Big Bear Sports Center
2618 King Ave. W.
Billings, MT 59102
406-652-5777
www.bigbearsports.com

Bighorn Fly & Tackle Shop
485 S. 24th St. W.
Billings, MT 59102
406-656-8257
888-665-1321 (toll free)
www.bighornfly.com

Eastslope Outfitters
(Main office)
1130 Nugget Pl.
Billings, MT 59105
406-254-6565
www.eastslopeoutfitters.com

Gart Sports Authority
100 24th St. W.
Billings, MT 59102
406-656-3888
www.sportsauthority.com

Rainbow Run Fly Shop
2244 Grand Ave.
Billings, MT 59102
406-656-3455

Scheels
Rimrock Mall
300 S. 24th St. W.
Billings, MT 59102
406-656-9220
www.scheelssports.com

Bozeman

Bob Ward & Sons
3011 Max Ave.
Bozeman, MT 59715
406-586-4381
www.bobwards.com

The Bozeman Angler
23 E. Main St.
Bozeman, MT 59715
406-587-9111
800-886-9111 (toll free)
www.bozemanangler.com

Fin & Feathers of Bozeman
81801 Gallatin Rd.
Bozeman, MT 59718
406-586-2188
877-790-5303 (toll free)
www.finsandfeathersonline.com

Greater Yellowstone Flyfishers
29 Pioneer Way
Bozeman, MT 59718
406-585-5321
www.gyflyfishers.com

Grossenbacher Guides
P.O. Box 6704
Bozeman, MT 59771
(406) 582-1760
www.grossenbacherguides.com

Montana Troutfitters
1716 W. Main St.
Bozeman, MT 59715
406-587-4707
800-646-7847 (toll free)
www.troutfitters.com

The Powder Horn
35 E. Main St.
Bozeman, MT 59715
406-587-7373

Rivers Edge
2012 N. 7th Ave.
Bozeman, MT 59715
406-586-5373
www.theriversedge.com

RJ Cain & Co. Outfitters
2201 Milwaukee Rd.
Bozeman, MT 59718
406-586-8524
866-378-7688 (toll free)

Yellowstone Gateway Sports
21 Forkhorn Trail
Bozeman, MT 59718
406-586-2076

A stealthy approach is often the key to success.
Photo by Brian Grossenbacher.

Butte

Bob Ward & Sons
1925 Dewey Blvd.
Butte, MT 59701
406-494-4452
www.bobwards.com

Fish On Fly & Tackle
3346 Harrison Ave.
Butte, MT 59701
406-494-4218

Fran Johnson's Sport Shop
1957 Harrison Ave.
Butte, MT 59701
406-782-3322

The StoneFly Fly Shop
2205 Amherst
Butte, MT 59701
406-494-0707
www.thestonefly.com

Cameron

Beartooth Fly Fishing
2925 Hwy. 287 N.
Cameron, MT 59720
406-682-7525
www.beartoothflyfishing.com

Galloup's Slide Inn
150 Hwy. 287 S.
Cameron, MT 59720
406-682-4804
www.slideinn.com

Wade Lake Cabins
P.O. Box 107
Cameron, MT 59720
406-682-7560
www.wadelake.com

Cascade

Prewett Creek Inn & Fly Shop
2468 Old US Hwy. 61
Cascade, MT 59421
406-468-9244
www.prewettcreekinn.com

Missouri Riverside Outfitters & Lodge
3103 Old US Hwy. 91
Cascade, MT 59421
406-468-9385
www.missouririverside.com

Clinton

Rock Creek Fisherman's Mercantile & Motel
73 Rock Creek Rd.
Clinton, MT 59825
406-825-6440
www.rcmerc.com

Columbia Falls

Arends Fly Shop
7356 Hwy. 2 E.
Columbia Falls, MT 59912
406-892-2033

Montana Fly Company
P.O. Box 2853 (mailing)
530 1st Ave. W.
Columbia Falls, MT 59912
406-892-9112
www.montanafly.com

Cooke City

Steelwater Outfitters
P.O. Box 1001
Cooke City, MT 59020
406-838-2267

Craig

Cross Currents
311 Bridge St.
Craig, MT 59648
406-235-3433
www.crosscurrents.com

The Trout Shop
110 Bridge St.
Craig, MT 59648
800-337-8528
www.thetroutshop.com

Darby

Bitterroot Fly Company
808 1/2 N. Main St.
Darby, MT 59829
406-821-1624
www.bitterrootflycompany.com

Dillon

Beaverhead Special
6590 High Ridge Rd.
Dillon, MT 59725
406-251-3337

Five Rivers Lodge
13100 Hwy. 41 N.
Dillon, MT 59725
800-378-5006 (toll free)
www.fiveriverslodge.com

Frontier Anglers
680 N. Montana St.
Dillon, MT 59725
800-228-5263 (toll free)
www.frontieranglers.com

Tom Smith's Backcountry Angler
426 S. Atlantic St.
Dillon, MT 59725
406-683-3462
www.backcountryangler.com

Uncle Bob's Outdoors
11 Pierce Dr.
Dillon, MT 59725
406-683-2692
888-683-RODS
www.unclebobsoutdoors.com

Divide

Great Divide Outfitters
871 Pumphouse Rd.
Divide, MT 59727
406-267-3346
www.bigholetrout.com

Emigrant

Hubbard's Yellowstone Lodge
287 Tom Miner Creek Rd.
Emigrant, MT 59027
406-848-7755
www.hubbardslodge.com

Matson Rogers' Angler's West
P.O. Box 4 (mailing)
Hwy. 89
Emigrant, MT 59027
406-333-4401
www.montanaflyfishers.com

Ennis

Madison River Fishing Co.
109 Main St.
Ennis, MT 59729
800-227-7127 (toll free)
www.mrfc.com

Montana Trout Stalkers
P.O. Box 1406
Ennis, MT 59729
(406) 581-5150
www.montanatrout.com

Tackle Shop
P.O. Box 625
127 Main St.
Ennis, MT 59729
406-682-4263
800-808-2832 (toll free)
www.thetackleshop.com

Fort Smith

The Bighorn Angler
P.O. Box 7578
Fort Smith, MT 59035
406-666-2233
www.bighornangler.com

Bighorn Country
Outfitters & Kingfisher
Lodge
P.O. Box 7828
Fort Smith, MT 59035
406-666-2326
800-835-2529 (toll free)
www.bighornkingfisher.com

Bighorn Fly & Tackle
Shop
P.O. Box 7597
Fort Smith, MT 59035
406-666-2253
www.bighornfly.com

Bighorn River Resort
P.O. Box 7595 (mailing)
Hwy. 313
1 mile north of Fort Smith
Fort Smith, MT 59035
406-666-9199
800-665-3799 (toll free)
www.forrestersbighorn.com

Bighorn Trout Shop
P.O. Box 7477
Fort Smith, MT 59035
406-666-2375
www.bighorntroutshop.com

Cottonwood Camp
P.O. Box 7667
Fort Smith, MT 59035
406-666-2391

Fort Smith Fly Shop &
Cabins
P.O. Box 7872
Fort Smith, MT 59035
406-666-2550
www.flyfishingthebighorn.com

Florence

River Otter Fly Shop &
Outfitters
5516 Old Hwy. 93
Florence, MT 59833
406-273-4858
866-800-4858 (toll free)
www.riverotterflyfishing.com

Gardiner

Park's Fly Shop
P.O. Box 196 (Mailing)
202 2nd St. S.
(US 89)
Gardiner, MT 59030
406-848-7314
www.parksflyshop.com

Great Falls

Big Bear Sports Center
121 NW Bypass
Great Falls, MT 59404
406-761-6400
www.bigbearsports.com

Montana River
Outfitters
923 10th Ave. N.
Great Falls, MT 59401
406-761-1677
800-800-8218 (toll free)
www.montanariveroutfitters.com

Scheels
Holiday Village
1200 10th Ave. S., #92
Great Falls, MT 59405
406-453-7666
www.scheelssports.com

Hamilton

Angler's Roost
815 Hwy. 93 S.
Hamilton, MT 59840
406-363-1268
www.anglersroost-montana.com

Bob Ward & Sons
1120 N. 1st St.
Hamilton, MT 59840
406-363-6204
www.bobwards.com

Chuck Stranahan's Flies
& Guides
P.O. Box 594
Hamilton, MT 59840
406-363-4197
www.chuck-stranahan.com

Fishaus Fly Fishing
702 N. 1st St.
Hamilton, MT 59840
406-363-6158
www.montana.com/fishaus

Harlowton

Ray's Sports & Western
Wear
Hwy. 12 & Hwy. 19
Harlowton, MT 59036
406-632-4320

Helena

Bob Ward & Sons
3323 Dredge Dr.
Helena, MT 59601
406-443-2138
www.bobwards.com

Capital Sports &
Western
1092 Helena Ave.
Helena, MT 59601
877-406-2978 (toll free)
www.capitalsportsmt.com

Cross Currents
326 N. Jackson
Helena, MT 59601
406-449-2292
www.crosscurrents.com

Montana Fly Goods &
Big Sky Expeditions
3180 Dredge Dr.
Suite A
Helena, MT 59602
406-442-2630
800-466-9589 (toll free)
www.montanaflygoods.com

Hobson

Trophy Trout Springs
Ranch & Fly Fishing
P.O. Box 167
Hobson, MT 59452
406-423-5542

Kalispell

Northern Rockies
Outfitters
270 Bayou Rd.
Kalispell, MT 59901
406-756-2544
www.northernrockiesoutfit.com

Snappy Sport Senter
1400 Hwy. 2 E.
Kalispell, MT 59901
406-257-7525
888-960-1234 (toll free)
www.snappysportsenter.com

Sportsman & Ski Haus
145 Hutton Ranch Rd.
Kalispell, MT 59901
406-755-6484
www.sportsmanskihaus.com

Lewiston

The Sport Center
320 W. Main St.
Lewiston, MT 59457
406-538-9308

Libby

Dave Blackburn's
Kootenai Angler
13546 MT Hwy 37
Libby, MT 59923
406-293-7578
800-322-9339
www.montana-flyfishing.com

Livingston

Armstrong Spring Creek
112 O'Hair Ln.
P.O. Box 955
Livingston, MT 59047
406-222-2979

Dan Bailey's Fly Shop
P.O. Box 1019 (mailing)
209 W. Park St.
Livingston, MT 59047
406-222-1673
800-356-4052 (toll free)
www.dan-bailey.com

George Anderson's Yellowstone Angler
P.O. Box 629
5256 Hwy. 89 S.
Livingston, MT 59047
406-222-7130
www.yellowstoneangler.com

Nelson's Spring Creek Ranch
101 Nelson Spring
Creek Rd.
Livingston, MT 59047
406-222-6560
www.nelsonsspringcreek.com

Spring Creek Specialists
2742 E. River Rd.
(shipping)
DePuy Spring Creek
(on-site shop)
Livingston, MT 59047
406-222-5664
www.sweetwaterflyshop.com

Sweetwater Fly Shop
5082 Hwy. 89 S.
Livingston, MT 59047
406-222-9393
877-628-3474
www.sweetwaterflyshop.com

Melrose

Great Waters Inn
P.O. Box 114
Melrose, MT 59743
406-835-2024
www.greatwatersinn.com

Montana Fly Company
P.O. Box 29
Melrose, MT 59743
406-835-2621
www.montanaflyco.com

Sunrise Fly Shop
472 Main St.
Melrose, MT 59743
406-835-3474
www.sunriseflyshop.com

Missoula

Bob Ward & Sons
3015 Paxson St.
Missoula, MT 59801
406-728-3220
www.bobwards.com

Blackfoot River Outfitters
P.O. Box 17182 (mailing)
3055 N. Reserve St.
Missoula, MT 59808
406-542-7411
www.blackfootriver.com

Brady's Sportsman Surplus, Inc.
Trempers Shopping Center
2315 Brooks
Missoula, MT 58901
406-721-5500
800-473-4867 (toll free)
www.sportsmanssurplus.com

Grizzly Hackle
215 W. Front St.
Missoula, MT 59802
406-721-8996
800-297-8996 (toll free)
www.grizzlyhackle.com

The Kingfisher
926 E. Broadway
Missoula, MT 59802
406-721-6141
888-542-4911 (toll free)
www.kingfisherflyshop.com

Missoulian Angler
802 S. Higgins
Missoula, MT 59801
406-728-7766
800-824-2450 (toll free)
www.missoulianangler.com

Wholesale Sports
2323 N. Reserve St.
Missoula, MT 59808
406-523-9000
www.wholesalesports.com

Ovando

Blackfoot Angler & Supplies
P.O. Box 84 (mailing)
401 Main St.
Ovando, MT 59854
406-793-3474
www.blackfootangler.com

Phillipsburg

Flint Creek Outdoors
P.O. Box 1063
116 W. Broadway
Phillipsburg, MT 59858
406-859-9500
www.flintcreekoutdoors.com

Nymph fishing is productive year round.
Photo by Brian Grossenbacher.

Pray

Knoll's Yellowstone School of Fly Fishing
P.O. Box 76
104 Chicory Rd.
Pray, MT 59065
406-333-4848
www.knolls.us/fishingschool.html

Red Lodge

Yellowstone Troutfitters
10 S. Broadway
Red Lodge, MT 59068
406-446-3819
www.redlodge.com/flyfishing/

Roberts

Beartooth Plateau Outfitters
HCR Box 1028
Roberts, MT 59070
800-253-8545
www.beartoothoutfitters.com

Ronan

Ronan Sports
63298 U.S. Hwy. 93
Ronan, MT 59864
406-676-3701
877-891-1425 (toll free)
www.sportswestern.com

Saint Regis

Clark Fork Trout & Tackle
226 Mullan Gulch Rd.
St Regis, MT 59866
406-649-2538
www.clarkforktrout.com

Saint Xavier

Bighorn River Lodge
P.O. Box 157
St. Xavier, MT 59075
406-666-2368
800-235-5450
www.bighornriverlodge.com

Royal Bighorn Lodge
P.O. Box 183
Saint Xavier, MT 59075
406-666-2340
www.royalbighornlodge.com

Tight Lines Lodge
P.O. Box 158
Saint Xavier, MT 59075
406-666-2203
406-666-2224

Stevensville

Backdoor Outfitters
P.O. Box 522
Stevensville, MT 59870
406-777-3861
www.backdooroutfitters.com

Troy

Kootenai River Outfitters
P.O. Box 775
1604 Hwy. 2 E.
Troy, MT 59935
406-295-9444
800-537-8288 (toll free)
www.kroutfitters.com

Linehan Outfitting Co.
472 Upper Ford Rd.
Troy, MT 59935
406-295-4872
800-596-0034 (toll free)
www.fishmontana.com

Twin Bridges

Crane Meadow Lodge
P.O. Box 489
Twin Bridges, MT 59754
406-684-5773

Four Rivers Fishing Co.
P.O. Box 395
201 N. Main St.
Twin Bridges, MT 59754
406-684-5651
888-474-8377 (toll free)
www.4riversmontana.com

West Glacier

Glacier Anglers
P.O. Box 210
12400 Hwy. 2 E.
West Glacier, MT 59936
406-888-5454
800-235-6781 (toll free)
www.glacierraftco.com

Glacier Wilderness Guides
P.O. Box 330
West Glacier, MT 59936
406-387-5555
800-521-7238 (toll free)
www.glacierguides.com

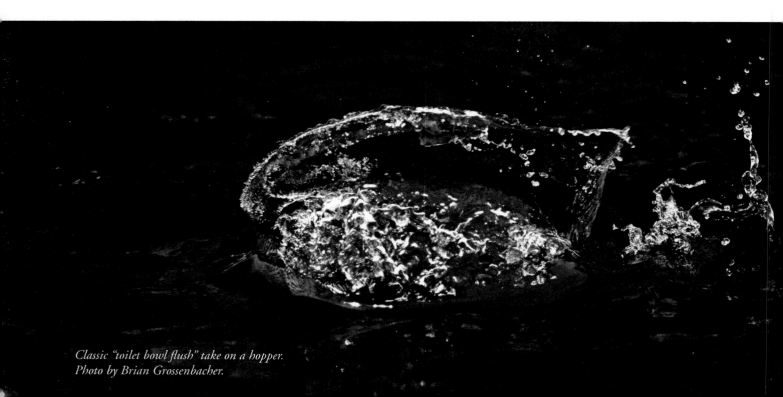

Classic "toilet bowl flush" take on a hopper.
Photo by Brian Grossenbacher.

West Yellowstone

Arricks Fly Shop
37 Canyon St.
West Yellowstone, MT 59758
406-646-7290
www.arricks.com

Blue Ribbon Flies
P.O. Box 1037
305 Canyon St.
West Yellowstone, MT 59758
406-646-7642
www.blueribbonflies.com

Bud Lilly's Trout Shop
P.O. Box 530
39 Madison Ave.
West Yellowstone, MT 59758
406-646-7801
www.budlillys.com

Eagle's Store
3 Canyon St.
West Yellowstone, MT 59758
406-646-9300
www.eaglecompany.com

Firehole Ranch
P.O. Box 686
West Yellowstone, MT 59758
406-646-7294
www.fireholeranch.com

Jacklin's Fly Shop
P.O. Box 310
105 Yellowstone Ave.
West Yellowstone, MT 59758
406-646-7336
www.jacklinsflyshop.com

Madison River Outfitters
P.O. Box 398
117 Canyon St.
West Yellowstone, MT 59758
406-646-9644
800-646-9644 (toll free)
www.madisonriveroutfitters.com

Whitefish

Lakestream Fly Fishing Shop & Outfitters
334 Central Ave.
Whitefish, MT 59937
406-862-1298
www.lakestream.com

Sportsman & Ski Haus
Mountain Mall
Whitefish, MT 59937
406-862-3111
www.sportsmanskihaus.com

Stump Town Anglers
5790 Hwy. 93 S.
Whitefish, MT 59937
406-862-4584
877-906-9949 (toll free)
www.stumptownangler.com

Wise River

Big Hole Lodge
36894 Pioneer Mountain
Scenic Byway
Wise River, MT 59762
406-832-3252
www.flyfishinglodge.com

Complete Fly Fishers
66771 Hwy. 43
P.O. Box 127
Wise River, MT 59762
406-832-3175
866-832-3175 (toll free)
www.completeflyfisher.com

Troutfitters
62311 Hwy. 43
Wise River, MT 59762
406-832-3212

Wolf Creek

Montana River Outfitters
515 Recreation Rd.
Wolf Creek, MT 59648
406-235-4350
800-800-4350 (toll free)
www.montanariveroutfitters.com

Conservation

No Nonsense Fly Fishing Guidebooks believes that, in addition to local information and gear, fly fishers need clean water and healthy fish. We encourage preservation, improvement, conservation, enjoyment and understanding of our waters and their inhabitants. While fly fishing, take care of the place, practice catch and release and try to avoid spawning fish.

When you aren't fly fishing, a good way to help all things wild and aquatic is to support organizations dedicated to these ideas. We encourage you to get involved, learn more and to join such organizations.

American Fly Fishing Trade Association ....(360) 636-0708
American Rivers..(202) 347-7550
Blackfoot Challenge..(406) 793-9300
California Trout..(415) 392-8887
Deschutes Basin Land Trust..(541) 330-0017
Federation of Fly Fishers ....(406) 585-7592
International Game Fish Association..(954) 927-2628
International Women Fly Fishers ....(925) 934-2461
New Mexico Trout..(505) 884-5262
Oregon Trout...(503) 222-9091
Outdoor Writers Association of America...(406) 728-7434
Recreational Fishing Alliance ....(888) JOIN-RFA
Rails-to-Trails Conservancy..(202) 331-9696
Theodore Roosevelt Conservation Partnership...(877) 770-8722
Trout Unlimited ....(800) 834-2419

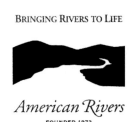

Cleaning up on DePuy's Spring Creek. Photo by Brian Grossenbacher.

More No Nonsense Guides

Fly Fishing Arizona
ISBN 978-1-892469-02-1
$19.95

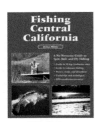

**Fishing
Central California**
ISBN 978-1-892469-18-2
$24.95

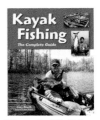

**Kayak Fishing
2nd Edition**
ISBN 978-1-892469-25-0
$24.95

Fly Fishing New Mexico
ISBN 978-1-892469-04-5
$19.95

**Fly Fishing
Southern Baja**
ISBN 978-1-892469-00-7
$18.95

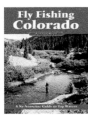

Fly Fishing Colorado
ISBN 978-1-892469-13-7
$19.95

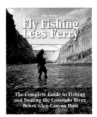

Fly Fishing Lees Ferry
ISBN 978-1-892469-15-1
$18.95

**Fly Fishing Central &
Southeastern Oregon**
ISBN 978-1-892469-09-0
$19.95

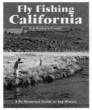

Fly Fishing California
ISBN 978-1-892469-10-6
$28.95

Fly Fishing Georgia
ISBN 978-1-892469-20-5
$28.95

**Fly Fishing the
Mid-Atlantic**
ISBN 978-1-892469-24-3
$29.95

Fly Fishing Utah
ISBN 978-0-9637256-8-4
$19.95

**Fly Fishing the
California Delta**
ISBN 978-1-892469-23-6
$49.95

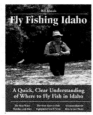

Fly Fishing Idaho
ISBN 978-1-892469-17-5
$18.95

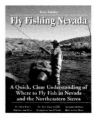

Fly Fishing Nevada
ISBN 978-0-9637256-2-2
$18.95

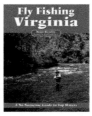

Fly Fishing Virginia
ISBN 978-1-892469-16-8
$28.95

Business Traveler's Guide To Fly Fishing in the Western States • ISBN 978-1-892469-01-4 • $18.95

Fly Fishing Pyramid Lake • ISBN 978-0-9637256-3-9 • $19.95

Seasons of the Metolius • ISBN 978-1-892469-11-3 • $20.95

Fly Fishing Magdalena Bay • ISBN 978-1-892469-08-3 • $24.95

*Mackenzie and Jenny Grossenbacher fish
Depuy's Spring Creek, Paradise Valley.*

Fly Fishing Knots

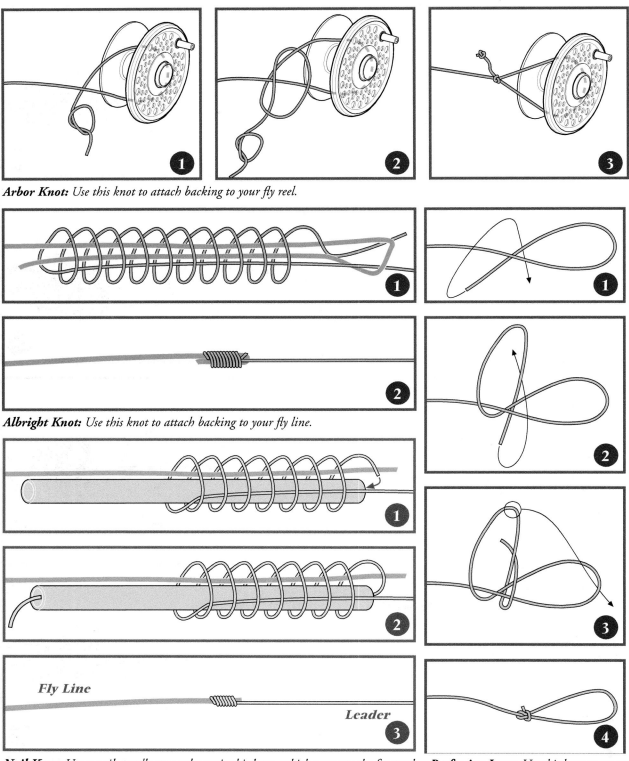

Arbor Knot: Use this knot to attach backing to your fly reel.

Albright Knot: Use this knot to attach backing to your fly line.

Fly Line

Leader

Nail Knot: Use a nail, needle or a tube to tie this knot, which connects the forward end of the fly line to the butt end of the leader. Follow this with a Perfection Loop and you've got a permanent end loop that allows easy leader changes.

Perfection Loop: Use this knot to create a loop in the butt end of the leader for loop-to-loop connections.

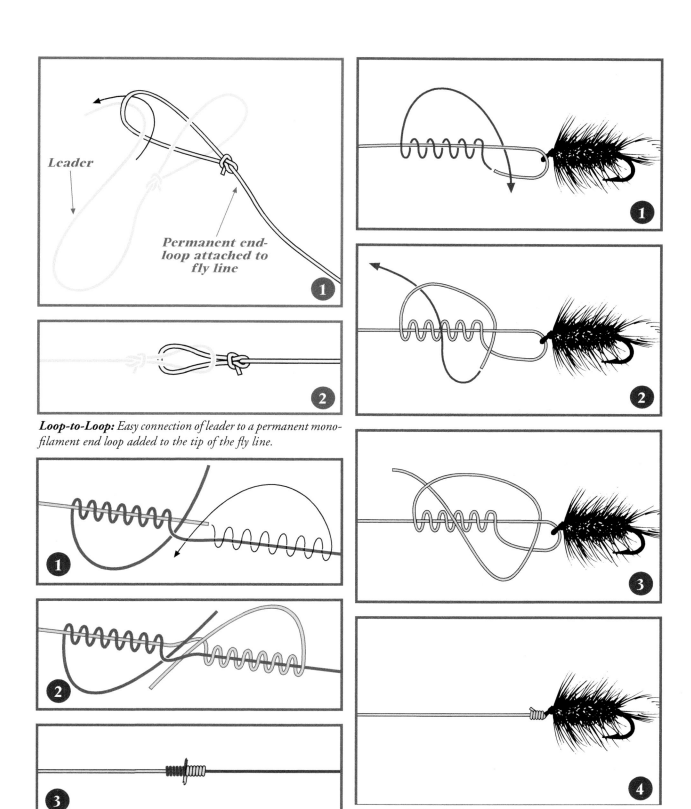

Loop-to-Loop: *Easy connection of leader to a permanent mono-filament end loop added to the tip of the fly line.*

Blood Knot: *Use this knot to connect sections of leader tippet material. Hard to tie, but worth the effort.*

Improved Clinch Knot: *Use this knot to attach the fly to the end of the tippet. Remember to moisten the knot before pulling it up tight.*

*The Absaroka mountains create a beautiful backdrop
for a jumping trout on the Yellowstone.
Photo by Brian Grossenbacher.*

The Grossenbachers each choosing the pick of the day. Photos by Brian & Jenny Grossenbacher.

Top Montana Fly Fishing Waters

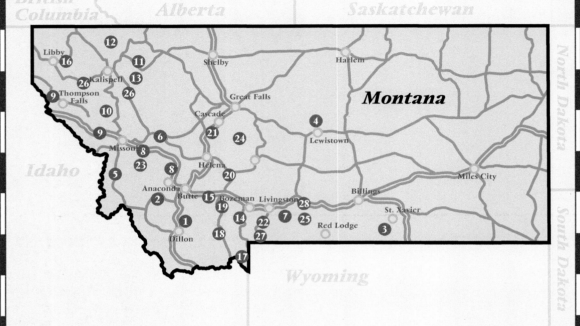

1. Beaverhead River
2. Big Hole River
3. Bighorn River
4. Big Spring Creek
5. Bitterroot River
6. Blackfoot River
7. Boulder River
8. Clark Fork, Warm Springs to Milltown Dam
9. Clark Fork, Milltown Dam to Idaho Border
10. Flathead River Main Stem
11. Flathead River Middle Fork
12. Flathead River North Fork
13. Flathead River South Fork
14. Gallatin River
15. Jefferson River
16. Kootenai River
17. Madison River, Yellowstone to Hebgen Lake
18. Madison River, Hebgen Lake to Ennis Lake
19. Madison River, Ennis Lake to Three Forks
20. Missouri River, Three Forks to Canyon Ferry Lake
21. Missouri River, Canyon Ferry Lake to Cascade
22. Paradise Valley Spring Creeks
23. Rock Creek
24. Smith River
25. Stillwater River
26. Swan River
27. Yellowstone River, Gardiner to Livingston
28. Yellowstone River, Livingston to Columbus